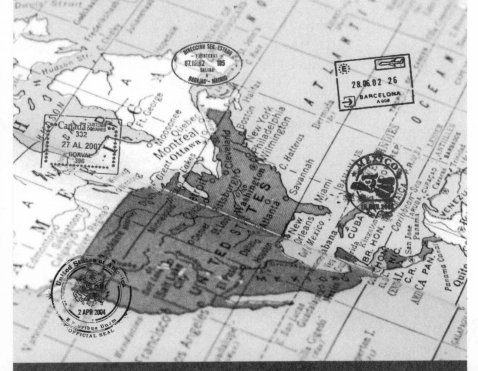

TWO GUYS
ON THE ROAD
Walking Backwards Across the World

Steve Chandler & Terrence N. Hill

Robert D. Reed Publishers   •   Bandon, OR

Robert D. Reed Publishers
P.O. Box 1992
Bandon, OR 97411
Phone: 541-347-9882; Fax: -9883
E-mail: 4bobreed@msn.com
Website: www.rdrpublishers.com

Editor: Kathy Chandler
Cover Designers: Angela Hardison and Cleone L. Reed
Typesetter: Debby Gwaltney

ISBN: 978-1-934759-63-9
ISBN 10: 1-934759-63-5

Library of Congress Number: 2012938997

Manufactured, Typeset, and Printed in the United States of America

To Kathy and Miranda, our traveling companions.

Introduction

The subtitle of this book is, admittedly, a little cryptic. But those who read our books with the attention that is, after all, only their due, will quickly recall Steve's offbeat exercise practice of walking backwards.

When I questioned him on this, he assured me that the Chinese have been doing it for millennia. And not only has it proven to do wonders for one's balance, posture, and breathing, but it also retrieves lost memories. Forgotten incidents and thoughts from your past will return to you as step by step you move backward through space and, apparently, time.

This theory struck me as having as much validity as that one about the moon and green cheese. In addition, my wife Miranda is Chinese and I've never once seen her walking backwards.

My skepticism led me to poke fun at Steve and his weakness for new-age, spiritually-based theories and ideas. I'm afraid I even did it quite publicly in our last book, which was written in 2009. I have since seen the error of my ways and have been forced to apologize to Steve for ever having doubted him.

You see the following year I made, with my wife and her family, my very first visit to China. Sticking to my usual discipline I started each day with a fast three-mile walk. Our first stop was Hong Kong and, consulting a map, I found there was a large park just a few blocks from our hotel. It seemed the ideal place to get in my three miles.

As I turned into the park I saw that I was not alone in seeking this as my exercise venue. The place was jumping, as were some of its visitors; others were jogging, working on martial arts moves, stretching, lifting weights, doing tai chi routines and – right there in the midst of all this, were a dozen or so men walking the park's broad central avenue *backwards*. Some walked in pairs and were talking, presumably relating long-forgotten anecdotes about how Mao used to crack them up during the famous "Long March" or maybe telling each other newly recalled incidents from their childhoods. So perhaps there *is* some validity to this walking backwards thing after all. Stranger things have happened ... though none really come to my mind right off.

Anyway, for some time Steve and I had wanted to write a travel book. It seemed a natural. We both travel extensively and when we get together or talk on the phone we often talk about the places we've been. We also both *enjoy* travel and seeing new places and things. Plus there's an interesting, built-in variety in the trips we take: Miranda and I travel primarily to other countries for pleasure and are free to stay longer periods, while most of Steve's trips are in the U.S. for business and tend to be for only a day or two.

Our working title – sticking with our valuable "Two Guys" brand – was *Two Guys on the Road*. We called it this without apology to Jack Kerouac because he's dead so what would he care? And we felt there was very little possibility of confusion with his book of a similar title because both Steve and I write so much better than he.

As the book started taking shape, it became clear that, as with the first four books in the "Two Guys" series, this one was as much about our lives and our shared past experiences as it was about the putative subject of the book – in this case the places we travelled to.

All writing is autobiography by its very nature. But it seemed to us that travel had a particularly strong tendency to bring back memories. My writing about a visit to Mexico City would remind Steve of his time in that city almost fifty years ago. Steve's business trip to London triggered thoughts of my time working there. And so on. In this way then, travel was producing the same recall effect as walking backwards.

The memories came back unbidden, but not unwelcomed. More disciplined writers might have ignored these random side streets and piloted their way right down the main highway of the subject at hand. Steve and I instead would immediately launch into a digression. And this digression might lead to another. And so instead of a traditional travel book we've wound up with something of a collage of places, people, opinions, travel tips and sometimes tenuously-related memories.

It was actually our publisher, Mr. Robert Reed, knowing what the book would be, who suggested the subtitle "Walking Backwards Across the World." And it seemed so right to Steve and me that, for the first time in recorded history, a publisher's suggestion was actually taken up by an author.

I've explained enough. Come with us; we're about to take a trip.

Terry Hill – New York, NY, USA
April 2012

1 January 2011 - San Miguel de Allende, Guanajuato, Mexico

Steve,

I am starting the year in San Miguel. Is it fair in what you and I have planned as a travel book to write about this town which could be considered my "home"? I mean we do have a home here. One in which we live four or five months a year. On the other hand, I do *travel* to get here.

I know that in conversation I tend to talk about San Miguel as a place where a lot of Americans, including Miranda and me, have come to live. This seems to put an emphasis on the highly-touted climate, the nice restaurants, the golf courses and the reasonable cost of living. Very much American retiree concerns. In fact the chief charms of San Miguel for Miranda and me are very Mexican. It's time to fill you in a bit.

The town, seemingly out here in the middle of nowhere, is *in* the middle of nowhere because there used to be silver here. Silver mining was the foundation of most of the early Spanish colonial towns in Mexico. Naturally, they worked the local Indians in the mines under awful conditions (there was no UMW of A in those days).

Priests came with the carpet-bagging Spaniards to convert the Indians, and with the priests came churches. It is the churches and convents that are the most salient architectural landmarks of the town today.

1542 is the official start date for San Miguel. I know this because we first came to the town in 1992 when they were celebrating its 450th anniversary. By the time the silver petered out, San Miguel had apparently achieved some kind of critical mass and managed to survive as a trade route center.

Its big moment came almost three centuries after its founding, in 1810, when a local grandee, Ignacio Allende, led the revolution that eventually won Mexico its independence from Spain. General Allende is thought of here much the same way George Washington is in the

States. With one important difference: Washington went on to be the first President of his country, while Allende never got that chance. He was captured by the Spanish and executed in 1811. His head was put on a pike and displayed for months in the nearby city of Guanajuato. Hell of a way to treat the father of the country.

The revolutionary heritage of the town made people aware of the need to preserve its historical ambiance. There are rather strict regulations governing what you can build, how high it can be, what materials you can use and what it can look like in the central part of town. (The paint-shade police are infamous here.)

There is a substantial Mexican visitor population year round in San Miguel, taking tours and visiting the scenes of their revolution in the same way an American might visit Boston or Philadelphia as the cradles of our revolution. On Fridays too at the Bar Azul in the Sierra Nevada Hotel you can see sugar-daddy Mexico City businessmen with their mistresses sipping Don Julio, no doubt here to learn firsthand the history of their revolution.

The preserved historical look of the town is also important because it was a contributing factor in the establishment in San Miguel of two art schools of some importance: Bellas Artes and the Instituto Allende. By the end of World War II both were in operation and drawing students and instructors.

Until the 1940s, San Miguel was very little affected by Americans, but that all changed with the GI Bill. This legislation, designed to educate the returning World War II veterans (and coincidentally keep them from glutting the job market for a few years) offered college expenses and a modest living stipend for any vet who wanted to pursue higher education.

The Instituto Allende was accredited and fully eligible for veterans to select. Quite a few did, many lured south of the border by the realization of how well they could live on their GI Bill stipend when they were spending it in pesos. This was the beginning of the American invasion.

Some of the veterans felt they'd landed in paradise and stayed on. Others went back to the States, realized they'd lost paradise and returned to regain it. Still others went back to the States and stayed back but while they were there, they talked about San Miguel as if it were paradise.

Word was up and running in the artistic and counter-culture circles and throughout the '50s and '60s, the town was known as a beatnik/hipster/hippie haven. Drinking, drugs and posing as artists were the major pastimes among the expat community. Neal Cassady, the charismatic but untalented Kerouac/Ginsberg/Kesey pal, died drunk here in 1969, still searching for a halfway decent sentence or another bourbon (which he figured were in the same place).

On the heels of the hippies, in the '80s and'90s, however, came Americans with money—a much more desirable class. And they've created their own version of paradise down here: Beautiful homes. Upscale shops. Health clubs and spas. Cable TV. Nice restaurants. And upgraded healthcare. Americans come here for a visit and fall in love with the place. Next thing you know, they're getting a guided tour of the town by a real estate agent.

Still, it's not a paradise for everyone and most of the expat residents fall into one of three major categories: 1) artists or would-be artists, 2) retired people, and 3) people of a temperament that allows them to pack up everything they have, leave familiarity and friends behind and start over.

A casual look at those groups will lead you to the suspicion that there may be many … shall we call them "eccentrics" here. Is this suspicion borne out? Well, let's just say that the chances of bumping into an eccentric while walking down *calle Zacateros* are pretty much the same as meeting a Chinaman in Shanghai.

All of which is okay with me; I'm rather fond of eccentrics, though, of course, I'm hardly one myself.

Terry.

7 January 2011 - Los Angeles, California

Dear Ter,

Kathy and I made our first trip of the year today. We flew in to LA to attend a fundraising dinner. I told Kathy on the plane that I'd recently read that Los Angeles County has a 44% high school graduation rate this year.

I remember when you and I went to high school in Birmingham, Michigan, graduation was close to 100%, but high school in 1962 meant more to a person's future.

I got an email from you this morning in which you mentioned Paul Stookey, of Peter, Paul and Mary fame, who had graduated from our high school I believe three years before us. He used to work at the Camera Shop in Birmingham. You pointed out that Stookey had made a record at Michigan State with running back Clarence Peaks! A few years ago Stookey mentioned Birmingham High School in his song, "Old Enough," in which he wrote, "Well I remember I was seventeen, I was a Birmingham High School rock and roll king / The paper talked about how I'd strut my stuff, I'd like to read it, but my arms aren't long enough."

Stookey's next verse brought him up to date: "I kinda like my new senior status, I don't even care what the latest fad is / My g-generation's rediscovered me, and now I'm on the cover of *Modern Maturity*."

S

8 January 2011 - San Miguel de Allende, Mexico

s.

Reading your LA note it occurred to me that most of your travel is for business. While none of mine is.

I miss business trips. There's something great about them. Somebody paying all your expenses to travel somewhere because you're needed *there*. Not your phone call, not your memo – you! It makes you feel valued, doesn't it?

Plus you get to go all these places you never would have gone to if it hadn't been "on business." And the places are always fascinating – to me anyway.

Yes, I know, it's almost a standard complaint that this or that job involves too much travel. That the travel gets you down. That it's stressful. Etc. But I've got to say that in my 30+ years in business I think I must have made something beyond 500 business trips (fewer than 20 per year at the start of my career, way more than that by the end). And I cannot remember a single trip I didn't enjoy. Now that's really saying something because I used to go to Ottawa a lot.

t.

1 / 11 / 11 - Gilbert, Arizona

Dear Terry,

Back home in Arizona where it's parched dry and kind of hot for January. I already miss the nice humid Pacific Ocean cloud layers of Los Angeles … and all the lush and effusive vegetation of the area. Always colorful and deeply aromatic … strangely calling to my mind Berlin, where I was stationed for a year and a half. I recall how the Germans loved to have flower pots everywhere and gardens and nicely tended walkways up to their homes, no matter how small the homes were.

By the way I agree with you on business trips. It's a kind of national collective victim story that says travel is a bad thing. When people talk to me they wince and moan when they hear how often I travel. But a few years back I decided to make travel a fun and relaxing affair. (Travel is only bad when you rush it. Which you could say about anything.) So I get to the airports early and put in my favorite music in my little musical headphone device and walk around. I don't rush and fret. I fly first class and if my business clients aren't willing to pay me the kind of fee that includes first class, I decline their request to do business. I want to arrive rested and focused, not a nervous wreck from having flown coach between two of America's obese people, all circulation gone from my arms and legs.

I also like to take my time coming home from a business trip. In the past I'd rush from the arena where I gave a seminar, suitcase in hand, to a waiting cab and then speed to the airport and be totally exhausted on the whole night flight home. Now I ease back to the room and don't leave till the next morning, filling my solitude with writing, reading and walking. (I've actually found that the more I slow down the more I get done.)

You are one of the few people who appreciate and enjoy business trips as I do. Most people want you to buy in to hassled, victimized and stressed-out stories about life. It's like a nation-wide victim club. (Didn't you once write a short story called "The Divorce Club?" I want to write one called "The Victim Club.")

And then when these victim people are dying they complain about how horrible it is that one has to die. Why is that horrible if all you did was complain about your life? People get into the habit of being victims and it runs their whole thinking process. It is the filter through which they see the world. The filthy glasses they wear to see everything. All my talks, all my books, all my work is to wake them up from this disgusting, ungrateful habit so they can live again like they did when they were kids running across the meadow, picking up lots of forget-me-nots. Everyone can feel like spring is sprung, if they would only learn to step back from their victim thinking and wipe it like sleep from their eyes because it is sleep. They are asleep to how beautiful life is.

    s.

13 enero 2011 - San Miguel de Allende, Mexico

Steve,

You say parenthetically that everything is better when you slow it down. I believe the 100-yard dash is an exception. And I believe the worldwide television ratings of the Summer Olympics would fall rather dramatically if next year the track people took your wisdom to heart.

I've just started a book called *A Reading Diary* by Alberto Manguel. It's very like one of our books in form: a year's worth of Manguel's reading and he comments as he goes. My first thought was that what was missing in the book (as compared to ours) is the dialogue – the back-and-forth. But after reading the first thirty pages or so I realize Manguel *does* have a dialogue – but instead of being with someone he's writing to, it is with the author of the book he is reading at the time.

However, I bring this up not because of similarity of our books, but rather because of his similarity to my situation in life. He was born and raised in one place (Buenos Aires) and has since moved to many places. He is now a citizen of Canada but, during the year of this book, is based in France but travels all over the world.

So where is home?

At the start of the book, Manguel is on a trip to Buenos Aires. It's clear he feels a deep recognition there. But I don't get the sense that he feels "home." And from my own experience being in foreign countries – more than half my life since the age of 20 has been spent outside the USA – I know you can never really feel at home in a different country/culture. You are always a guest. I suspect Manguel feels what I feel – that he is a man without a home.

This is not meant to be dramatic or a plea for sympathy. The fact is I very much enjoy this situation. Writers are always, to some extent, on the outside looking in. They almost have to be. And this condition of not having a home more or less formalizes this position. Because you're *always* on the outside.

I know I've told you in the past that the time I feel most "home" is when I'm in the Midwest. But whenever I'm in Michigan now, I know I long ago gave up having that place really be "home." So maybe "home" isn't quite right, maybe I mean most in touch with my roots.

Yes, there are major psychological drawbacks to not having a "home." But it keeps you on your toes. And I'd rather be on my toes than in an easy chair.

t.

January 20, 2011 - Beverly Hills, California

Dear Terry,

Greetings from Beverly Hills where we are visiting a couple of days just for fun. Today we took a tour of movie stars' homes in Beverly Hills and Bel Air. You talk about feeling at home; I wondered how many of these stars could really feel at home in such heavily manicured walled-in fortresses. We drove by Tom Cruise's house and it was mainly blocked from view by huge hedges.

The last time we talked, you mentioned visiting Birmingham and re-walking your old *Detroit Free Press* paper route. You mentioned an obscure Elvis song from one of his many odd movies, *Kissin'*

Cousins. In that movie he sings a song about going back to the home he loves. But in the movie *Kid Galahad* Elvis sings "Home Is Where The Heart Is." And to follow the theme of the song, your heart would be anywhere Miranda was. So now you're always home.

I almost put "New Prospect, New Jersey," up atop this letter instead of Beverly Hills because that was the setting for John Updike's book called *Terrorist* that I finished at the hotel. (A great writer like Updike can put you there, so you are even more there than here!) Quite an amazing book! My theory is that it was Updike's answer to Tom Wolfe who had called him out a couple years before for being a washed up irrelevant old *artiste*.

Updike was born twelve years before you and I were, in 1932, and as this riveting, compelling novel about home-grown terrorism in America proves, he could write with as much punch at 73 as he could when he was 20. Heartening! Home is where the heart is, and my heart was in that book. Old man, take a look at my life!

s.

ps. Kathy was happy that we were bumped to First Class because of my many accumulated miles traveling, even on the short flight from Phoenix to L.A. it makes a difference in comfort, and it also takes care of a phobia of mine, listed in the medical journals as Fear of Flying Coach.

23 January 2011 - San Miguel de Allende, Mexico

Steve,

Then, of course, there's always Robert Frost's: "Home is the place where, when you have to go there, they have to take you in." A rather depressing notion from a man, who, it appears to me now, rather specialized in depressing notions.

When I was younger I always used to have this notion of Frost as a kind New Englander with a wry sense of humor and a twinkle in his eye. But then a few years ago there was a biography of Frost which seemed to suggest the man was a total jerk. So then my impression changed to a petty, spiteful man with a *malicious* sense of humor.

Recently, however, I read a book of Frost's letters. In one letter, talking about writing, he says: "I own any form of humor shows fear and inferiority. Irony is simply a kind of guardedness. So is a twinkle. At bottom the world isn't a joke. We only joke about it to avoid an issue with someone. Humor is the most engaging cowardice."

It's possible that someone may convince me otherwise at some point, but right now I'm pretty firm in suspecting that Frost was not only a jerk, but a morose one totally without a sense of humor. Saying that people *with* a sense of humor are cowards is merely a mask for Frost's own lack of the same. But by the ultimate irony, I now consider Frost a joke.

Actually I do like a lot of his poems, especially the early narrative ones from his book *North of Boston*. Did you know that Frost taught at the University of Michigan for a time? As did, by the way, former Poet Laureate of the U.S. – Donald Hall.

Terry.

January 25, 2011 - Gilbert, Arizona

Ter.

Could it be that Frost's name subconsciously made him so frosty and humorless? How could he denounce humor? On the other hand, perhaps there are more people like him than like us. We who see humor day to day versus those who never see it. Maybe we should call this book *Two Cowards Travel the Planet*.

Frost! What made him think that way? Living in the snowbound northeast?

Steve.

6 February 2011 – Merida, Yucatan, Mexico

Steve,

Merida. Not a place I expect you and Kathy are likely to ever get to. I've been here for three days now and I give you my official permission to miss it. Don't get me wrong, I'm glad to have been here for three days but today I'm saying *adios* to Merida, not *hasta luego*.

The place is falling apart. A crumbling ruin in the middle of the Yucatan jungle. And it's hot! So hot and humid that you wonder why anyone would ever choose to live here. Anyone! Especially a conquistador before the days of air conditioning! Those conquistadors were lucky that they had horses, that they had muskets and that someone had conned the Indians with that famous prophesy that a tall god would arrive in Mexico in a certain year because otherwise I don't think they could have pulled it off – the conquest I mean. Because honestly those conquistadors could not have been too smart. The evidence is that a number of them settled in Merida. Not clear-thinking men.

The city is now almost a million people and I don't see how any of them is able to accomplish a single thing ever in this wet, wet heat.

You know what I love about being a writer, Steve? Obviously a rhetorical question because I'm sure you feel the same.

It's all about telling stories. It's not about "art" or even about "truth." It's about that one day when you write/tell a story so vivid and interesting that whoever reads or hears it wants to tell it to the next person he meets or to his wife and kids or to his friends. The story may be fiction or truth, or a little of each, but it is so interesting or compelling that it demands to be passed on. Hopefully, of course, there will be royalties for the writer. But more important, there is immortality.

Or at least as close an approximation of immortality as we can ever really hope for. Writers create stories that, if they're lucky, live beyond their obituaries.

So now I'm going to tell you a couple of stories that were told to me here in Merida. In this envelope I have enclosed a small packet with two grains of salt, one of which you may take with each of these stories.

Still I find the stories so interesting that I have to pass them on. And perhaps god put me on earth to do just that.

Legend has it that when the first conquistador landed on the Yucatan peninsula, he approached the local chieftain and asked him: "What do you call this place?"

The chief answered, "Yucatan." Which in Mayan means: what did you say?

I've heard this story four times now over a period of several years and each teller told it with a straight face. It is a great story, don't you think? But to me it has the whiff of apocrypha about it. On the other hand, I am so rooting for the story to be true that the next time I tell it, I will announce it as gospel. And, as everyone knows, if a story is told often enough unchallenged, it will eventually be accepted as truth. And once it reaches that status, the actual truth is irrelevant.

The second story is curiouser and is the explanation of a major oddity in Yucatan cuisine. If you look at a few menus in restaurants serving Yucatecan food you will notice that a number of their signature dishes feature Edam cheese as a key ingredient.

Edam is the cheese you see in the red-wax covered balls in cheese sections of supermarkets or specialty cheese shops. It is made in Holland. So how did it get to be so much a part of the Yucatan? If it had been a Spanish cheese, one could understand, but the Dutch have otherwise almost no presence here in Mexico.

Apparently in the late 1800s, a ship from Holland, bound for the Dutch West Indies, ran into a storm in the Yucatan channel and was wrecked on the Mexican coast. Included in its cargo were hundreds of boxes of Edam cheese in their traditional wax and red cellophane wrappings which protected them from the sea.

Soon afterward, Edam cheese balls started turning up on the shelves of Merida grocery stores. Many in the Merida upper-crust had spent time in Europe and knew what this cheese was and how to use it in cooking. And thus was born the Edam-based Yucatecan dishes that are mainstays in Merida today.

Miranda and I tried two of these dishes and were not overly impressed, but after having heard the shipwreck story, how could we resist?

Footnote: have you ever read a novel by Compton Mackenzie called *Whisky Galore*? (It was also made into a movie which I've never seen, but was supposed to be quite good.) The novel takes place during World War II when whisky (yes, they spell it without the "e" in the UK, and in Canada too for that matter) was rationed. In the novel a ship carrying cases of whisky runs aground and has to be abandoned off the coast of Scotland. Thirsty locals sneak on board and relieve the ship of some of its contents with comic results. I wonder if the Yucatecan Edam fetish story started after MacKenzie's novel came out in 1947.

Adios, Merida. Off to Chichen-Itza and Valladolid tomorrow.

Terry.

7 February 2011 - San Diego, California

Terry,

I'm in San Diego reading your message from Yucatan, and I have to say thanks for the salt. I'll take it when I get home.

I am here in the land of the Padres to give counsel to a client of mine who owns and runs a design agency. I found out when I arrived, looking at the colorful artwork on the walls of the clients his agency serves, that the baseball Padres are a client of his.

Therefore I chose not to share with him all the withering comedic satire I wrote about the Padres' name in the baseball book we wrote. That's the problem with these edgy, no-holds-barred books we write, you never know who will be offended next.

But I won't back my style down. The gloves are still off, and I don't even care if I lose *all* my clients, starve to death, or have to finish our last chapters from a jail cell … I will make this book our edgiest yet because this time we are here to critique the earth itself! And its many overrated destinations.

But I'll praise, too. John Updike said that our only job on this earth was praise. Therefore I now declare comedic ridicule to be a form of praise. From now on if you start to feel its sting, or if any city does, know I'm praising.

arises we are willing to recognize the loyalty and monetary outlay of our readers by offering them the benefit of some of our experience and wisdom. I believe we should be willing to "give something back" as the currently popular phrase goes. And we should do so *even* if it means sharing an experience that doesn't show us in the most glowing possible light. It's the kind of unselfish act that I am willing to do.

Okay then, readers, let me just say that the joys of travel are great, but there are also some drawbacks, some things you should watch out for. One of these is the obvious fact that, especially on a tour like this, you are sleeping in an unfamiliar bedroom every night.

Just so that our readers get a clearer picture of what I am about to relate, let me start by saying that I sleep in my jockey shorts. You were probably wondering. The particular shorts in question are maybe a couple of years old and – as happens when we get old – they sag a bit. Miranda has several times in the last half year suggested that I throw them out. But there are no holes in them yet so I see no reason to do so.

And so it happened that on our night in Valladolid, sleeping in this unfamiliar bedroom, I woke up at about 2:30 in the morning needing to go to the bathroom. I made my way to the room door, opened it and started down the hotel corridor in search of a restroom. I've already described the hotel as a bit of a maze, and one corridor led to another then up a few stairs and then another corridor but still I couldn't find a bathroom.

You are probably wondering why I didn't just use the bathroom in our room. The answer to that should be obvious – I was still asleep. However, after several minutes of wandering the hallways I was gradually awakening and realizing my position:

I was walking the corridors of this maze-like hotel in the middle of the night wearing only my droopy underpants. I also had to go to the bathroom. I figured there must be one somewhere near the hotel's restaurant so I started moving in that direction. But when I got close I could hear a couple of people in the kitchen talking to each other and I backed away.

My thinking on this was that I was not sure I could explain myself in English at this point and a Spanish explanation was clearly beyond my abilities. Still, my need for a bathroom was growing more urgent. I walked down to the end of one of the corridors (I wasn't at all sure where I was at this point) and found a trash basket lined with a black plastic bag and figured that this was going to be about as good a substitute for a bathroom as I was likely to find at this hour. So I made use of it.

Now some of the sleep-fog was lifting from my brain. I knew that I'd closed my room door behind me and I was thinking that I'd have to go to the front desk and ask, with as much self-possession as I could muster, for a second key to room 321. There were several problems with this plan: the first you've probably already worked out, I clearly wouldn't have been able to produce any identification if asked. The second, however, was the nagging uncertainty as to whether it really was room 321 ... or was it 312?

I had an alternate plan, which also had problems, but they seemed slightly less daunting. I went back to my room, 321, and tentatively started knocking. I didn't want to knock too loudly for fear of waking someone in one of the adjacent rooms, but I had to be loud enough to wake Miranda in the room ... or should I be knocking instead on 312?

Fortunately, after a minute or so I heard Miranda's voice on the other side of the door asking who it was. "It's me," I stage-whispered. "Let me in." Once safely in our room I gave Miranda an abbreviated explanation of what had happened, got back into bed and tried to get to sleep again. It isn't all that easy to get back to sleep when the person on the other side of the bed keeps breaking into uncontrollable giggles every few moments.

And so, readers, I leave you with this very valuable travel tip:

Before you go to bed in your hotel room, it's a good idea to put a couple of chairs and maybe also your luggage in front of your door as a barricade. Not to keep intruders out, but rather to make it difficult for you to slip out the door in your underwear.

neighborhood in 1906 after having been away for two decades. In short, Hank was pissed off. He hated all the changes that had been made in the intervening years and went off on a rant that produced much the same feeling as listening to one of those guys you run into now and again who can talk for a blistering half hour about how major league baseball has been ruined by the designated hitter rule. Let's face it though, James was a bit of a stuffed shirt. And I don't think I'm alone in coming to this conclusion.

So to put forward a contrarian point of view on this, part of what I love about New York is how much and how rapidly it *does* change. Don't get me wrong, I love the traditional too. Like having lunch with you at a bar that's been pretty much the way we saw it since 1854 (except that now they allow women). Like all the old tenement buildings downtown and the brownstones uptown. Like the White Horse Tavern and the Four Seasons. And the Brooklyn Bridge and the Flatiron Building. But the thing about New York is that every year there are a hundred – no, I lie, *a thousand* – new things, restaurants, bars, music places, cafes, shows, whatever. All there to go to, to see, to test, to taste, to experience. No other city can touch it. And I've been to – and lived in – a lot of great cities.

All of which is a long way of getting around to: How could you have possibly "forgotten how great New York is?" I guess you can tell I'm kind of missing it right now.

Terry.

5 March 2011—Mesa, Arizona

Hey Terry!

I traveled to Mesa tonight with Kathy to see Gunnar and Matt Nelson at the Arts Center perform a tribute to their father Ricky Nelson.

You and I talked before starting this book about weaving a little music into it. Because I know we both see these books someday ending up on Broadway, with handsome actors reading our exchanges back and forth. And great music behind them. And your point was that there are many songs about traveling and being on the road (again).

Last night I thoroughly enjoyed myself as the Nelson twins, singing well and playing bass and guitar with surprising skill and verve, sang Ricky's greatest hits while taking numerous breaks to show us film clips of the *Ozzie and Harriet* show and Ricky's concert footage. I had tears in my eyes more than once going back in time to when you and I were young.

I remember that you had introduced me to Fats Domino whose "Blueberry Hill" was a hit as well as his bouncy, "I'm Walkin." Ricky Nelson's first recording was "I'm Walkin'" with "A Teenager's Romance" on the other side of the vinyl.

Tears came to my eyes when they played a moody, harmonically beautiful version of "Lonesome Town." Prior to playing it, they showed a clip of Paul McCartney talking about how big Ricky Nelson was in England and Europe, and how good his records and vocals were. He especially liked "Lonesome Town," and I remembered that Paul has recorded that song.

Then, of course, "Travelin' Man" was played, and although it's a very pleasant Top 40 kind of song, I caught myself wondering if it could be sung by a woman. Could a woman sing proudly about having a lover in every city in the world without the lyric sounding "slutty?" It was considered, in Rick Nelson's 50's and early 60's, cool for a man to "own," as the song says, "the heart of *at least* one lovely girl" in every port in the world. I've added the italics there. The suggestion is that it's not a girl in every port. It's *at least* a girl in every port. That's the minimum.

Pretty Polynesian babies, sweet frauleins in Berlin town, etc. all around the world. What if a woman were that same "Travelin' Woman?" Would we admire her as much? Or would we have a doctor look at her prior to engaging in a serious relationship? Just asking.

I'm not making any larger point. I'm not saying I agree with every female I know who says all men are pigs. I'm just asking about a particular hit song.

Another beautiful song sung by the twins tonight was Rick's hit "Teenage Idol" in which we hear, "I travel around, from town to lonely town, I guess I'll always be just a rolling stone."

Just a rolling stone? I thought it was good to be a rolling stone. So good you'd even consider naming your group the rolling stones. It's funny how music treats the idea of travel. On the one hand, there's the loneliness of it. There you are out there like a rolling stone, with no direction home. Like a complete unknown. But then there's the romance and glory of being a rolling stone that gathers no moss. Here's to you my ramblin' boy, may all your rambling bring you joy.

All this brings up a question I have always had listening to folk songs and rock songs. It's a question about something it seems everybody knows about but me. Maybe you know about this, Terry, and if you do you can tell me. It's something called "the line." Ricky Nelson had a song I always loved called "Down the Line." It has a wild energy to it and I can play it over and over without tiring of it. But I never know what "the line" is. He sings, "I'm gonna move on down the line, I'm gonna get some love that's truly fine ..."

Fred Knipe (our friend, comedian, award-winning songwriter, four time Emmy-award winner for TV writing, etc.) and I used to sing the blues folk song "Walkin' Down the Line" with great gusto and good harmony. But I never knew, even while singing from my heart, what "the line" was.

Is it a railroad line? A lineup of women? Maybe you can help me with this. Is it the line on the highway that the cop asks you to walk when you've had too many to be driving?

I think if we are going to sell ourselves as the sequel to Kerouac's *On The Road*, as two modern guys on the road, we'll need to know what the line is. Is it perhaps the line from birth to death? Maybe I'm reading too much into it. But my greatest fear is that I may be reading too little into it. I've always had that vague worry that there's some fundamental thing about life that I don't understand. Something so simple that even Ricky Nelson and Johnny Cash ("I walk the line") understand it. Something that may even be the key to the understanding of life itself.

Can you help?

S.

7 March 2011 – San Miguel de Allende, Mexico

Steve,

I note that in your last letter you refer to Rick(y) Nelson several times as Ricky and other times as Rick. This is something I've wrestled with myself: What to call Eric (his real first name, by the way) Nelson. I mean I'd be lying if I said it was my biggest problem in life, but it's probably in the top ten.

I do remember his conscious effort to have himself called "Rick" instead of "Ricky," which I thought was a bit silly on his part. In writing, I can awkwardly resolve it (as you've seen) with the unwieldy "Rick(y)." But what about when I say his name out loud? I'll try to work out some solution before the next time I see you in person.

On "the line" issue, I must admit I'm as in the dark as you. But no time like the present, I thought. Let's get this sorted now! So I went to the internet, which as you know, is now the solution to *all* problems.

I googled the Bob Dylan song you mentioned – "Walkin' Down the Line." And the first thing that pops up are about twenty YouTube versions of the song. Everyone's done it – Dylan of course, Joan Baez,

Linda Ronstadt, Arlo Guthrie and Pete Seeger and tons of others. But the one that caught my eye, and that I checked out, was a truly embarrassing version by none other than Eric "Rick(y)" Nelson.

It's from a performance on the Merv Griffith show. Rick(y) (who Merv introduces as both "Rick" *and* "Ricky") is dressed in a suit and tie. He could be on his way to a job interview, but instead he's lip-synching to a Bob (by) Dylan song. Since there's no band on stage, and yet you're *hearing* a band, the director was obviously desperate to come up with something to show during the instrumental break. The solution he hit upon was not a good one – from out of nowhere come a couple of young guys also in suits who kind of shuffle-dance with Rick(y) while a banjo is playing … somewhere. It's very weird and you're left with a vague suggestion that perhaps Rick(y) had a gay side to him.

In the end, though, I was glad I saw the clip. Because even though it turned up no clues to "the line" mystery, it did remind me of a great lyric in the song that I'd forgotten:

> "I see the morning light
> Yes I see the morning light
> It's not because I'm an early riser
> I just didn't get to sleep last night."

The line reminds me of a stanza about travel in a William Carlos Williams poem:

> "I have discovered that most of
> the beauties of travel are due to
> the strange hours we keep to see them."

Before we erase "the line" from our thoughts, let me remind you that Rick(y)'s father, Willie, played so vividly on television by a guy named Ozzie, also wrote and sang a "line" song – "Farther Down the Line." A song about a rodeo rider. Almost all rodeo songs are travel songs, by the way. Ian Tyson's written a bunch of them, most notably "Someday Soon," and they're all about ramblin'.

I believe that my favorite travel song is "Fort Worth Blues." It was written by Steve Earle as a tribute to Townes Van Zandt and it mentions nine different cities and states in it. That's a far cry from Hank Snow's "I've Been Everywhere," which mentions 92 different place names! But the Hank Snow song doesn't have the philosophy inherent in Earle's verse:

> "You used to say the highway was your home
> But we both know that ain't true
> It's just the only place a man can go
> When he don't know where he's travelin' to"

But, when I start thinking about it, there are so many good traveling songs.

How about Woody Guthrie's "I Been Doin' Some Hard Travelin'?" Or another Woody song "Ramblin' Round?" It has the line "I never yet saw a girl I liked as I go rambling around."

This last thought almost directly contradicts another Guthrie traveling song "More Pretty Girls than One." ("Every town I ramble 'round / there's more pretty girls than one")

Frankly, in my experience, the second song is the truer. In fact, I'd go as far as to say that the existence of so many pretty girls has been one of the major distractions of my life. I can't tell you how much smoother my life path would have been if all the intelligent women in the world looked like Bella Abzug and Golda Meir. Unfortunately an awful lot of them looked like Susan Sontag.

Steve, I know you've been calling me Terry for 55 years or so, but I'd like to request that you stop. From now on would you please call me Ter? Much appreciated.

t.

10 March 2011. Napa. California

Ter,

Back when I drank for a living I would have been a wild man here in Napa touring the vineyards and "tasting" the various samples. As it is now I soberly follow the guide as he walks us through the massive caves of barrels and I make mental notes about all the subtleties of winery. I'm thinking I can use some of this information in our book.

I step outside the cave, though, and a glorious visual storm of green floods my senses … green grass, green trees, green fields kissed by the sun. Living in Arizona, especially the valley we live in, does not accustom the eyes to such a riot of green, green as the green of life itself … overwhelmingly beautiful to one used to an oppression of sand.

I was here in Napa to do work with my client, the wonderful Napa School of Music. It was a good day of work with people thoroughly dedicated to bringing music into the lives of as many people as possible. I love music. You love music. You introduced me to much of the music I love now … and you did that in the 1950s.

One spooky and cool thing about Napa is that they have a wine train running through town. This would have inspired more than one song in my songwriting days. A wine train! What a metaphor for an alcoholic's long, strange ride. What a train to ride.

I was never a wine connoisseur. My most favored wine drink was white port and lemon juice. But I did not raise my hand on the sophisticated winery tours and ask about white port and lemon juice. It was a famous ghetto drink. A great doo wop song about it was called WPLJ … and Frank Zappa later covered that record.

This Napa valley is as beautiful a place as I have ever been. Where is the most beautiful place you have ever been? I used to say, for me it was Hailey, Idaho. Now I will replace it with Napa. What's your nomination?

S

14 March 2011 – San Miguel de Allende

Steve,

What *is* a travel book? I know it's kind of an embarrassing question to be asking at this point when we're already steaming along writing one, but it's been a bit of a bug in my brain lately.

The central issue in my mind is: is it the journey? Or the destination? The trip or the place? I think about some of my favorite travel books, and in many of those, the answer's easy – they're clearly about both.

For instance everyone raves about Bruce Chatwin's *In Patagonia*. And you won't catch me arguing against its status as a travel classic; I loved it. Clearly it's about both the trip and the places he visits.

But what about a book like *A Year in Provence*? There's very little travel in it; it's very much about place. And yet I'd definitely put it in the travel section of any bookstore. Because it's about discovery – the discovery of place. And isn't that pretty much what we like about travel?

I know this is all kind of academic because we're going to write the book we're going to write and we're going to call it a travel book no matter what. But just as an organizing principle I think that's the definition I'm going to keep in my head: it's about the discovery of place. Some of that discovery has to do with the experience of getting there. But travel itself is very much about discovery. Even – as much as I deplore the whole fad – *self* discovery.

There used to be a lot of conflicting opinions about what was the worst movie ever made. But that was before *Eat Pray Love* came out. Now there's no question. Some people might argue with me on this, but I can tell their hearts aren't really in it. (These arguments generally come from women who seem to do heart flips over Javier Bardem and his funnily-shaped nose. Don't get me wrong, I take great heart from his popularity, having – I've been told – a funnily-shaped nose myself.)

I have a friend who, after having seen it, has always referred to the film as *Eat Pray Vomit*. There is simply way, way too much self-discovery in the film, and sappy self-discovery at that.

I've not read the book the movie's based on, but I can't believe it's as bad as the film because I've seen video clips of the author speaking and she struck me as at least a borderline plausible human being. I suppose you could classify hers as a travel book too, though doing so makes me nervous that we seem to be writing a book in the same category.

Still the best parts of the film (the only good parts) were the travelogue bits, especially in Italy before Julia Roberts truly lost it in her own navel. And it was these parts that proved for me our eternal fascination with travel. So okay, okay, I'm *glad* we're writing this book.

t.

17 March 2011 - San Diego, California

Ter,

I'm back in San Diego for another meeting. The news reports today said that there might be radiation from Japan blowing across the Pacific onto the California coast. I don't care. A little bit of radiation might even be a benefit to me since I never go to doctors to get checked for cancers. Maybe I have cancer and this little bit of radiation will be all I need to keep it in remission until we finish this book.

I agree with you about *Eat Pray Love* being a perfectly awful movie. However! I think your loathing of self discovery is based on a misperception. This movie wasn't about true self discovery, which I find to be a brave and honorable pursuit. But rather the false confusion of self-fascination and narcissism with self discovery and spirituality. As practiced by Julia's character, it is almost the opposite of true self discovery.

And speaking of "progressive" confusion, while in Napa we stayed at a nice inn but when we went to put the "Do Not Disturb" sign on the door handle we found that it said "STILL ENJOYING THE ROOM." Was there a problem with "Do Not Disturb"? I know this is California, but this was ridiculous.

But not as ridiculous as the "Do Not Disturb" sign they have for my door here at the Marriott Courtyard in San Diego (California). This sign says: "I NEED SOME ME TIME!" You probably think I am kidding but I am not. Kathy thought I was kidding when I called her from the hotel last night to tell her about this door hanger. So I am bringing the sign home to prove it to her.

Eat Pray Love is a terrible travel movie, and it actually should have been called *I Need Some Me Time*. Self-indulgence confused with self-discovery.

The great French poet Charles Peguy said it – and I'll translate this from the French for you … oh, I forgot you speak French – but maybe our readers don't, and actually maybe I don't either, so here is what the French poet said, which I think is appropriate to the *Eat Pray Love* narcissist/protagonist who leaves her good husband in search of great food and sex under the umbrella of self discovery … Peguy said, "It will never be known what acts of cowardice have been motivated by the fear of not looking sufficiently progressive."

S

18.March.11 – San Miguel de Allende, Mexico

Steve,

I hope you realize – given our comments on *Eat Pray Love* – that after this book's published, Julia Roberts will never speak to us again. We may want to reconsider. Is it worth losing a potentially valuable friend (not that either of us has met her yet) merely for the sake of telling the truth?

The most beautiful place I've ever been? Obviously a hard one. Your choices suggest beautiful landscapes, and though I've never been to Hailey, Idaho, I'm willing to trust your judgment (or eyes) on that. Because I *have* been to Napa and agree that it's pretty spectacular.

But I must say my taste runs more to the manmade ... to cityscapes. And if I had to decide what I'd like to look at one last time before pulling an Oedipus on myself, I'd go stand in the middle of the Pont de Sully in Paris, the section of the bridge that goes from Ile St-Louis to the Left Bank, and look toward Notre Dame. The Left Bank's on your left, Ile St-Louis on your right, the Seine below and flowing out toward Ile de la Cite and Notre Dame with its flying buttresses in full flight. Tough to beat for me.

By the way, I think you're being unduly hard on Arizona. The first time I was ever there, out visiting you in 1971, I had much the same reaction you expressed about the unrelenting beigeness of the landscape. But after being there only a few days and seeing the mountains at different times of the day in different light, I changed my mind. It's not a lush beauty like Napa or Vermont, but it's an austere beauty that inspires a certain amount of awe.

You're just too used to it.

t.

19 March 2011 - Gilbert, Arizona

Terry,

You are right. Arizona is very beautiful. And I get too used to it. So when I go somewhere green it's amazing. That's really the beauty of travel. Two guys on the road. Seeing this planet with fresh eyes and feeling an almost childlike sense of wonder, as I did in Napa.

Country singer Rex Allen Jr. wrote and recorded a great song called *I Love You Arizona.* You can youtube it. The Superstitions he refers to are mountains near my home:

> "I love you Arizona,
> Superstitions and all;
> The warmth you give at sunrise;
> Your sunsets put music in us all."

S.

21 March 2011 – San Miguel de Allende

s.

This book started for me on December 31, 1986. Miranda and I went out for a year-end dinner at a restaurant in the Village that no longer exists called Vanessa on the corner of Bleecker and 7th Avenue. During the dinner I put forward a proposition. We both loved travel and at that point in our relationship we'd already been on trips to the West of Ireland and to France together. But wonderful as those trips were (as *all* trips are to me), we both felt that what we missed on vacations like these was a sense of what it would be like to *live* in these places.

We'd seen Galway Bay and the Eiffel Tower. But what would it be to wake up every morning in a cottage on the Aran Islands or in the shadow of the Tower? What would it be like to have half the people in your local pub speaking Gaelic or having a daily morning routine of café au lait and croissants on the terrace of a café reading the *Herald-Tribune*?

I wanted to live in a lot of different places. I wanted to live in each one long enough to get a sense of the local. I wanted to know more than just the Paris sites and monuments, and their dates and histories;

I could get that from a guide book. I wanted to know at which cafes musicians hung out, or writers, and where to go for oysters on the half shell and a bottle of dry white wine to waste a Thursday afternoon. And where to get the best baguettes in the neighborhood, *my* neighborhood. And maybe most of all I wanted to do all this with Miranda.

Here was the proposition: With New York as a base, each year we'd take off for somewhere – Paris, Santa Fe, Lisbon, Santiago, Tuscany, anywhere we wanted. We'd get an apartment or a cottage and live there for three to five months and really get to know the place. Then we'd return to New York until the next adventure. All this time I'd be writing and Miranda would be doing whatever she wanted to in whatever place we were – studying, cooking, doing crossword puzzles, painting or something she'd not even thought of yet.

Well, of course, the missing element in this plan was money. We'd never be able to live that life and still have jobs, at least the kind of jobs we had then. Jobs that we very much enjoyed, but which wouldn't let us live the peripatetic life my proposition imagined. So, we'd have to retire, but then we'd have no bi-monthly paychecks to pay for it all.

I then took out a piece of paper with a lot of numbers on it. A financial plan. It started with a budget showing how much we'd need each month after we'd retired. Then there was a number indicating how much capital we'd need to generate that much each month if we weren't working. And then I showed how over the next five years we could get to that number though savings, investments, the sale of some properties we owned, etc.

It was like a mini-business plan. The kind of thing you show on a lap-top in a PowerPoint presentation across a desk to your banker to get his buy in. But instead it was a plan for a shared life on a piece of notepaper shown across a dinner table at Vanessa to Miranda to get *her* buy in.

My fear was this: Miranda was just 32 at the time and on a fast track in advertising. She had "potential CEO" written all over her. Would she be willing to pack it all in and wander off to some Marco Polo life that was just in my mind right now? Especially in five years time when she'd be even closer to a top spot? So I ended my pitch by asking if she'd be willing to do this, something nobody else we knew had ever done anything like. And would she be too disappointed not to wind up her career as the head of some big agency?

I remember her answer exactly.

"The only thing that would disappoint me is if you don't make this happen."

Five years later we had a four month lease on a two-bedroom stone cottage in San Miguel de Allende, Guanajuato, Mexico. Miranda found the place in a small classified ad in *New York Magazine.* At the time she knew so little about San Miguel that she asked me which ocean it was on.

San Miguel is almost exactly in the middle of the country about three and a half hours north of Mexico City by bus. And pretty much equidistant from the Atlantic and the Pacific.

In 1992, it was hard to get to, hard to get out of, hard to call, and call *from,* by telephone. There was no internet then and our "cottage" didn't even have a television, a VCR player (remember VCRs?), or water you could drink. The local movie theater played a pretty steady diet of kick-boxing movies in Spanish, a language we didn't speak.

It was totally different from anything we'd ever lived before. But for the first four months of that year, we lived it ... and, I must say, loved it. Our traveling life had begun.

More to come.

terry.

25 March 2011 - Marina del Rey, California

Terry,

I am here in Marina del Rey where I often meet with my California clients. The Marriott always gives me a wonderful conference room high up on the seventh floor overlooking the marina filled with boats, and further out you can see the Pacific ocean.

Most conference rooms I work in are claustrophobic, which isn't always bad given that my business goal is usually to replicate the feel of an Israeli Mossad interrogation. But it's beautiful here.

What you have just written gives depth and philosophical poetry to your lifestyle. Many people envy you and Miranda for your constant travel, but don't fully understand it. Many see it as post-retirement wanderlust. Or a desire to follow in the footsteps of Hope and Crosby. But I love what you just wrote ... the underlying sense of purpose and especially the desire to really *experience* the places you visit.

When I teach my clients self discovery I like to distinguish the difference between being a human being and a human doing. The difference between taking creative action and just being busy. Human *beings* are you and Miranda and the way you travel.

I know you think you despise self discovery, but it's because you are already discovered and have no need of it. You are living it through travel and of course have no desire to "learn it," and especially not at the level of eating, praying and trying to love Julia Roberts.

Many people I know use travel as a distraction. An escape. A way out. But then they find that when they arrive at their destination, they are still there! Shoot! Same mind, same thoughts, different setting.

A worried man will be worried wherever he goes. And it takes a worried man to sing a worried song. (Wisdom you turned me on to in 1955.)

Last night Kathy and I watched a film by Lixin Fan called *Last Train Home*. It's a documentary about China and it is absolutely, quite colorfully mesmerizing. It made me want to go to China. How close is a film to reality? What is reality? I know you two went to China this past year yourselves. So watch the movie and tell me about it. I have always loved China, (my latest book was inspired by Bruce Lee ... America's bridge to China.)

Didn't you take a slow boat over there?

S

ps- One of the many great things about good movies is that they can give the viewer a sense of travel. They can visually and sensually put the moviegoer on the road.

3 April 2011 – leaving San Miguel for Mexico City

Steve,

Miranda and I have had a 25-year running disagreement about the proper time to arrive at a bus station. This disagreement, I might add, extends also to train stations and airports. But let's take bus stations as an immediate case in point.

It is my contention that the proper arrival time is hours before the stated departure time. Miranda, on the other hand, is an advocate of just-in-time arrival. Her rationale being, why waste time sitting in a bus station waiting? "That's why they call them 'waiting rooms,'" she kindly points out as if I'd not already known, or at least guessed at, the derivation of the term.

My point (and it's one I must admit I've never put forward to Miranda because I find that women often get a bit huffy in the face of a truly logical argument that happens to contradict their "feelings") is this: what are you going to be doing at home during this time? Do you have a State of the Union message to prepare? Or maybe you were going to just dot a few "I"s and cross the "T"s on your paper announcing the cure for cancer? No, the fact is you'll be reading a newspaper or your detective novel. Which is *exactly* what you'll be able to do at the bus station.

Except that at home I'm unable to read the newspaper or my mystery because I'm too worried about possibly missing the bus/train/plane. Miranda calmly points out that we've always arrived in plenty of time for our departure and, yes, I admit that this is true ... *so far*! But what if the U.S. is unexpectedly on Code Red and it takes six hours to get through security? What if the bus left early? These things can happen, Steve; I've read about them.

Okay I will admit that in the entire history of Mexico not a single bus/train/plane has ever left ahead of schedule. On the other hand, I'm sure you've heard the expression: There's always a first time. Yes, I know it's a cliché, but do you know why clichés get used so often? Because they're often true!

I believe I've made my point, so I'll leave it at that. Except to conclude by saying that the result of this difference of opinion is what amounts to a negotiation over what time we should leave for any station or airport.

Bottom line: Miranda has finished not just one, but almost two *New York Times* crossword puzzles in the San Miguel bus station while we've been here waiting to go to Mexico. She's just given me a look that says, basically, "Well here we are."

(Just a bit of a footnote. A lot of you probably thought I made a mistake when, in the last paragraph I wrote "Mexico" instead of "Mexico City." In fact, Mexicans always refer to the city as just "Mexico." If they're talking about the country, it's usually clear from the context. It took me about three years living here to get used to this. Someone would say he was going to take the bus to Mexico, and I'd be thinking, "Wait. Aren't we already *in* Mexico?")

My father always loved Mexico City. Living and working here for two years, he found the city rough-edged, exciting and full of life. This was a few years after World War II and the city's population was under 3 million. Today it's over 20 million. It really is one of the most interesting and vibrant cities in the world. This is why when Miranda and I fly to Mexico (the country) each year, we usually do *not* fly to the airport closest to San Miguel.

The closest airport would be Leon, about an hour and a half drive from San Miguel. But we prefer to fly to Mexico City which is almost a four hour drive from our home. There are several reasons for this seemingly illogical choice but the primary one is that we like to spend a few days enjoying Mexico City at each end of our stay in the country.

Today we have a new reason for coming to Mexico City – a brand new major art museum: the Soumaya, just opened to the public last week.

According to *Forbes* magazine, the richest man in the world is a Mexican industrialist named Carlos Slim. Now I have never been the richest man in the world so what I am about to say is based on what I would call intelligent conjecture rather than actual experience, but I suspect that the richest man in the world has a lot of friends. I would also be willing to bet you than every single one of those friends either has – or hopes to have – some kind of financial tie to him.

After you lost that bet, you probably don't have much left to bet against me again, but I would also be prepared to wager that every single person in the world who does *not* fit into the "friend" category will dislike the richest man in the world. All of these people will be looking for the chance to say something bad about him. This is probably why the richest man in the world, no matter who it might be at any given time, will often tend to be a little reclusive, to be kind of private and hang out almost exclusively with his friends. (Think Howard Hughes.)

This makes sense. Why be out rubbing shoulders with the public, when 99 out of 100 of the people who own those shoulders dislike you, whether they've ever met you or not? And why stick your neck out when there are millions of people who are just waiting for the chance to cut it off?

In other words, Carlos Slim was just asking for it when he announced he was going to open a major new art museum to house his family's art collection. The Soumaya Museum opened in Mexico City last week and was greeted by savage reviews in the press. It's hard to feel sorry for the richest man in the world, but even though I agreed with much of the criticism, I didn't quite feel he deserved the blasting he got.

I mean, don't we want to encourage the richest man in the world to channel some of his billions to art for the public? Maybe the review could have said: Well, that one didn't quite work, but nice try, Chuck; and, by the way, thanks for making the entrance free to the public.

Miranda and I were outside the museum within half an hour after checking into our hotel. There was a line of people waiting to enter the museum, so long that we had to walk a couple of minutes before we could even see the end of it. After standing in the line and watching its progress, it became clear that it would take 45 minutes to an hour before we'd get to the door. I avoided the bulk of this wait by a strategy you too might find useful, Steve:

I played the age card.

Well, technically I suppose, I didn't play it, it played me. We were standing in the line when a young Mexican with some kind of official-looking badge on walked up to a cane-using old woman, maybe 75 or 80 years old, and began talking with her. I'm not sure exactly what he said because she was maybe six or seven people in front of us in line, plus, as you may have suspected, my Spanish isn't *that* good, but the sense of it was clearly: "Because you are pretty much on life-support and we'd like you to see the entire show before the arrival of the Grim Reaper, you can go to the head of the line and get into the museum now."

This is obviously an impressionistic translation of what he said. A more slavishly exact translation might have read something like, "People 60 and older can go to the head of the line."

Recognizing this, it was at this point that I made myself and my codger status visible to this guy. He responded by waving me forward. Miranda came with me, trying to give the impression that she was a nurse or serving me in some care-giving capacity. Which, I suppose, she does.

We made our way to the head of the line and then entered the museum some 25–30 minutes earlier than we would have had I been seven years younger.

The museum itself is striking from the outside, looking like a huge gleaming sculpture. It has been described as resembling the tail of a giant whale diving ... well, I suppose if you squint.

Inside, we went by elevator up to the 6th floor and then walked down ramps to each lower floor, an idea apparently patterned after Frank Lloyd Wright's Guggenheim Museum in New York. The improvement in the Soumaya is that you are not required to look at art while standing slanted downward as you are at the Guggenheim. Here the ramps merely get you to a lower floor; there is no art hung on the walls of the down ramps. Both Miranda and I find it less disturbing to look at paintings when you aren't bothered by the notion that you might tip over.

We saw all six floors and, as I suggested, there's a lot wrong with the museum: there is, for instance, no obvious flow to guide you through each floor, so you always have the sense that you've missed things. Usually, in fact, you have. Meaning that you are constantly backtracking to get to an area you unknowingly passed.

There is also a problem that the collection seems unfocused. On one floor, almost side by side, you might have a Monet landscape, display trays of old coins, framed stock certificates, antique pianos and anonymous 19th century family portraits. A bit of a jumble with no real explanation that I could see. Still, most of the collection is art, and while you can argue that the quality is uneven, there are certainly some very fine pieces. Quite a few actually.

Nice try, Mr. Slim.

t.

4 April 2011 - Gilbert, Arizona

Terry,

Kathy and I have the same difference of habit on the issue of arriving early for a travel departure, or even a movie. She, like Miranda, does not like sitting around waiting. On the other hand, I love it. Like you, it reassures me that I have already arrived safe and sound in my own future. No possibility of missing a bus or plane or show. To Kathy's credit, she has met me halfway. She agrees to arrive somewhat early. But she always brings a book, and she has a device on her phone that can shine a light on her book in a dark theater.

In fact that "phone" of hers doubles as a computerized internet television with connections to the entire universe. It's a profoundly complex device (while I carry a simple phone) and if she wants to, if sitting and waiting is boring enough, she can hack into the Pentagon or text with international celebrities while waiting for our show to begin.

I, myself, lived in Mexico City when I was 18. I had been banished for a year from the University of Arizona, and so I took a bus from Detroit to Mexico City and lived there instead, ostensibly learning Spanish. The reason I was kicked out of college was grades. I missed all my final exams. I got drunk during exam week at a motel in the desert where I had taken a room to "study."

A friend and I got so drunk that we decided to write, compose and stage a water ballet in the motel pool for the entertainment of the other guests sitting around the pool. As you know, I am not a great swimmer, and this ballet was a real disaster, even though we worked very hard creating it.

Regardless, that ballet got me to Mexico City, and I loved that. I even returned to the University a year later and resumed my "education" without any more evictions. Twelve years later, I was a proud graduate.

In Mexico, I lived in a boarding house where only Spanish was spoken, took Spanish classes and drank a lot. I was an alcoholic but I didn't know it. And I hadn't hit the real depths of consumption back then.

It was 1963 and I had a nasty housemate and one day when he came in to my bedroom to tell me my president had been shot I thought he was just taunting me with inappropriate humor until later that evening when I heard street vendors who were selling papers yelling "Kennedy Asesinado" and "Kennedy Muerto"

Things weren't as dangerous on the streets of the city back then. I was truly young. There was romance and adventure for a 19-year-old.

Your mention of the bus ride reminded me of all the times I've traveled through that Mexican countryside. So often we used to travel by bus or train from Tucson to Puerto Vallarta or Mazatlan or just Nogales. Even the dead horses are beautiful, in the right frame of mind.

Like William Carlos Williams (as you quote in your March 7th letter) I've also always felt that most of the beauties of travel are due to the strange hours we keep to see them.

It's funny that when my mind is dull and weary and full of worry it sees the world the same way. I see everything wrong with the world. But when I'm refreshed and illumined on the inside, I start seeing how good people are to each other. How everyone wants to help everyone else. When I visited you in Mexico I saw this spirit of help everywhere. Except for the one incident. When our airport shuttle van backed over a crippled guy sitting on a sidewalk. We didn't exactly kill him (and I saw someone rushing to his aid) but we didn't start his day off in the best possible way. That I was pretty sure of.

Miranda told Kathy on that trip that when the two of you decided to retire and to travel that you really wanted to travel authentically, into the heart of the countries you were seeing. I almost said into the heart of darkness, but it's more like you're going into the heart of the light. That kind of travel polishes the glass of observation.

Polish the glass, and you'll see more. A lot of people thought that J.D. Salinger's great character in fiction, Seymour Glass, was named because of that idea. "See more glass." He was a seer, a poet and a modern day saint. When I was young and reading Salinger I used to wish more people were like that. Back then I thought people had permanent personalities and finite characters and they were either like Seymour or they weren't.

What I'm glad I've learned since is that we can all be like that. We can all see more. We can all polish the glass and see more. We can all have the illumined mind that Emerson speaks of and with it we can see that the whole world sparkles with light. It doesn't sparkle with light all by itself. Which was Emerson's point. It sparkles with light when you shine the right mind on it.

You didn't *have to* take a bus to the land of Kidnap Kab Co. and the beat cop known as Machine Gun Kelly. But you did. So you're like the Steve Miller band: "Pack my bags! Goin to Mexico!" (Always my favorite song of his.)

Writing about my college hiatus in Mexico, the irony hit me. YOU, my friend, were a super-motivated high achiever. You graduated from college in four years! You got a law degree. I could go on and on. I failed at everything. I was one of the greatest underachievers who ever lived. It took me those 12 years – 12 YEARS – to get my bachelor's degree. And my army career was no better. When I was discharged, I was a Private! Four years of service, and I leave a Private! Maybe our readers are not familiar with the ranking system in the army, but that is not super achievement.

Yet I am the one writing books and giving seminars on *achievement*. Well. It's probably too late to change any of this.

    S

8 April 2011 – NYC, NY, USA

Steve,

Half awake this morning I was thinking I was still in San Miguel, but when I opened my eyes I was greeted by a wonderful rainy New York 7 AM.

Weather isn't something that affects me as much as it seems to other people. Yes, it's nice to have a beautiful day in New York. But a chilly, rainy day's fine by me too. I certainly wouldn't move out of the city because of the weather. When I'm living in New York, I'm there because of the city not because of the weather.

That holds true for San Miguel too. I love the old colonial look of the town, the need to at least *try* to speak Spanish plus the food, the restaurants, the churches, the markets, the culture, the cantinas, the characters – the whole *mezcla*. Weather would rank below all of those things in a list of reasons I live here.

On the other hand, it was awfully nice to wake each morning in Mexico to blue skies and an 80-degree day.

Getting here from San Miguel is … I was going to write "hard," but maybe "wearying" is more the right word. It's not really arduous, but it *is* about twelve hours door to door. Cab to the Mexico Airport, flight from Mexico City to Dallas, customs and immigration in the Dallas airport followed by a layover there, then the flight from Dallas to New York, and finally a cab to Bleecker Street and home. The cab picked us up at 9 AM Mexico time and we got here at 10 PM New York time (which was 9 PM in Mexico).

I actually like plane rides. (Outside of "turbulence," which, even when it's mild, scares me to death.) Generally I just hunker down in my seat with my book or magazine or my writing and have this sense that I'm getting something done. Miranda always packs good food and does a *New York Times* Sunday crossword, occasionally asking my help on the sports or literature clues and therefore making me feel vaguely as if I'm earning my French bread and whatever cheese she's brought in her provisions bag.

My big problem on flights is my addiction to whatever movie they're showing. Unless it's a film I've already seen it'll generally take me about two lines of dialogue before I'm into the story and hooked. On the Dallas-NYC flight I watched a film about a mermaid. I'm generally not really big on mermaid films as a genre, and in New York it wouldn't have even made my maybe-see list. But on the plane, within a scene I was into it.

It was called *Aquamarine* and featured about ten actors I can almost guarantee you've never heard of. Later I looked up the director on the internet. Her only previous directing credit is a film about a loser high school wrestler who wins his first match when his glass eye pops out and stuns his opponent to helplessness. (I know, I know, you think I'm making this up, but that's what it said. I'd give a lot to have been in the room when that movie was being pitched to the studio.) Apparently she did such a good job on this glass eye film that when the mermaid script popped up *six years later*, they immediately thought of her.

Obviously I received a lot of trash talk from Miranda for watching this thing. And I acknowledge deserving it. Especially since I quite enjoyed the film. Still, as addictions go, I don't think bad-movies-in-planes is quite as dangerous as heroin, right?

t.

9 April 2011 – Gilbert, AZ

Terry,

That thing about the glass eye had me howling. And not that I didn't trust you, but I looked up the director and discovered you weren't lying.

One of the things airlines might think about is that a frequent flyer will be offered the same film on every flight of the month. About five years ago, for instance, I remember seeing *King Kong* three times in three weeks ... oh I never watched it with sound; it was just up there, but one can't help sneaking glances. And I noticed that the female lead in the movie, Naomi Watts, never once, in any scene she's in, closes her mouth. I'm not joking. Because of the airline's movie schedule I verified this observation twice.

s.

11 April 2011 - Washington, DC

Terry,

Kathy and I are here in the nation's capitol seeing all the sights on a true vacation. Most of our past "vacations" have been business trips for me that we add a day or two to see the sights. But this is pure vacation.

And I'm pretty excited because I don't know if you have ever heard of this big thing called the Lincoln Memorial, but it's a huge statue of Abraham Lincoln seated in a big stone chair inside an amphitheater with his famous speeches carved into the walls. Stunning!

The reason I ask if you have heard of this memorial is because it is obviously brand new to Washington. How do I know that? Because everyone, and I mean *everyone* (including Kathy) is taking pictures of this thing. There must not be any pictures of this yet anywhere because people are extremely eager to take their own pictures of it.

I don't know if you are a camera guy, but I am not. Kathy is, and I am not. In fact I'm not much of a visual person. Kathy is very visual. You can tell that right away by looking at the two of us on any given day. The way she dresses versus the way I dress. It's clear that she values the visual and I really don't.

Here's the downside, though, of traveling with someone with a camera. It's like walking a dog who has to urinate every two minutes. You stop the walk and let the dog urinate. A camera person stops over and over and if you are with her you stop too. A hundred times a day. On a vacation like this.

Here's my hypocrisy in this: I am the guy who later begs her to show the pictures of our vacation up on the big screen so I can do a comic narration and win over family members with my wit. She does all the work; I jump in when it's an advantage to me. She has identified a lot of that in our lives.

We got a tour, just the two of us, of the Capitol building by an intern in our congressman's office. He was a wonderful young man who took us all round the building. I had been reading David McCullough's great book *1776* on this trip, so the historical sites meant more to me because of the power of that book to make everything so real.

Tomorrow we are spending the day at Mount Vernon, the home of George Washington. I look forward to that.

S.

12 April 2011 - Washington, DC

Terry,

First a garden tour on the lawn of the White House. As we walked up to the house itself I noticed a dog behind me on the path and I said to Kathy, "They let dogs come in here with the tourists?" Security had been strict coming in and I couldn't figure it out.

Kathy said, "Maybe it's a guide dog." But this dog was walking loose, and it was a big furry thing, hardly the look of a guide dog. Then I saw someone very close to the White House call to the dog and the dog lazily walked past us up onto the lawn and then into the White House itself! It was President Obama's dog, Bo!

Soon we were aboard a Grayline tour bus to Mount Vernon, the home and farm of George Washington. The driver gave us nonstop running commentary. It occurred to me that he could be making everything up. I pictured myself taking over a tour for a day and making all the facts up for the tourists. "Across the way on the other side of the river on the left you'll see the little cottage that Thomas Jefferson and his mistress Tawana used for weekend getaways."

Mount Vernon was a beautiful spread of land and we walked all around it. Down by the river, up the hills, and finally into Washington's home itself where there were Stepford-scripted women stationed in each room telling us about the history of the rooms. We finally got to the bedroom where George Washington died, and I remember the woman describing it in ways that were disturbingly graphic. Pointing to his bed, she told how he suffocated, choked on his own vomit or something, while the oxygen was leaving his lungs and his thrashing and gulping for air were to no avail as the father of our country expired in a sweaty heap. Kathy and I both thought 1) she may have been making all this up, who knows why? Maybe because she herself was having a really boring day. Or 2) it was true, but why do we need to know it?

Mount Vernon's blooming gardens contained lots of hollyhocks and when we got to the gift shop Kathy bought some straight-from-George-and-Martha's-garden hollyhock seeds. To plant in our own back yard in Phoenix. So that we could start with those hollyhocks to perhaps recreate the whole feel of Mt. Vernon at our little house in Arizona.

When I saw the packet of hollyhock seeds I said, "Awkward."

Why did I say "awkward"? Back in the old days when you and I were boys in the early '60s I used to listen to Rod McKuen records where he read his own poetry with music in the background. I loved those records. I think one was called "Listen to the Warm." Isn't that beautiful? And although he was often mocked by the fierce contemporary (real) poets who believed him to be a moron, I loved his sweet words and music. And right here in the Mount Vernon gift shop his poetry drifts back to me. (Not being a garden or outdoors guy I had not heard the word *hollyhock* since listening to that record.)

> *You stand*
> *among the awkward hollyhocks,*
> *little breasts and big eyes,*
> *love's machinery not yet working.*

Love to Miranda, S.

22 April 2011 – New York City

Steve,

During the writing of each of our previous books I've come to a moment when I've been struck by the thought that nothing we're writing could possibly be of the least bit of interest to anyone. Well, I came to that moment sometime last week. I'd pretty much convinced myself that this is going to be the most boring travel book ever written.

At about this time I started reading Alain de Botton's *The Art of Travel*. I found it an incredibly uplifting book because I am now absolutely certain that we are *not* writing the most boring travel book in history. It has already been written by Mr. de Botton.

This book drew very good reviews and I can't understand why. Because it's impossible that a writer this dull could have that many close friends on both sides of the Atlantic. For the benefit of our book I've undertaken an analysis of why de Botton's book is so uninteresting.

One of the problems I think is that de Botton doesn't seem to like travel much. At one point he goes to Madrid on what is basically a business-related trip but he doesn't want to leave his hotel room. There he is with all of Madrid to explore and he wants room service. He's finally forced out because the maid wants to clean the room.

But the major reason for the dullness is that the author is incapable of having an interesting thought on his own. Fortunately he is sometimes able to recognize other people's interesting thoughts and his book benefits from liberal use of quotations.

The Art of Travel is promoted as a book that will tell you the "how and why" of travel with sort of a philosophy 101 overlay. In fact the book is made up of essays on a variety of other subjects with usually the most tenuous possible connection to travel. For instance, there is an essay on Vincent van Gogh very loosely tied to a trip de Botton made to Arles. There's another on John Ruskin's thoughts on the possibilities of the possession of beauty; the only connection with travel seems to be a reference to Ruskin's belief in travelling slowly. An essay on Wordsworth is linked to a trip de Botton takes to the Lake District, but after reading it you realize the whole essay could just as easily have been written without ever taking a single step out of his London home. (To make a dull essay even duller he quotes many lines from Wordsworth's poems. Wordsworth was the Rod McKuen of his day.)

As for the philosophical overlay, I'll give you one example:

At one point de Botton is wandering in the Lake District with a companion through the great outdoors. They watch a bird on a pine branch. Imagine the excitement when it then … flies away. Without the bird to entertain them, they turn their attention to a caterpillar crawling across a rock. (I'm not making this stuff up.) At the climax of this walk, a sheep grazing nearby wanders over and looks curiously at them. They look back at him. And it's here that de Botton gets deep on us: "What makes me me and him him?" he asks.

At this point I knew I was in over my head.

Terry.

23 April 2011 - Tucson, Arizona

Terry,

We are in Tucson to attend the wedding of the daughter of our friends, Nina and Tim Daldrup.

Tucson is a much more colorful, cultural, bohemian, counter cultural city than Phoenix. It's closer to Mexico, and so the architecture is more charmingly Mexican, whereas Phoenix is always trying to be a kind of barren, modern version of California.

The wedding was at the zoo! And it was outdoors on a charming green where a very good three piece bluegrass band played as guests milled about. Soon we were invited to a private feeding of the giraffe! I can promise you this would never happen in Phoenix. You just wouldn't have the people with the imagination to do this, nor would the Phoenix zoo indulge it.

While relaxing here in the Old Pueblo, I read your piece on Alain de Botton. Sounds like that book is a must to avoid. But I got the unsettling feeling that de Botton sounds a little like me. I have a hard time describing things. I am not a very visual person. Kathy always negotiates a hotel room with a great "view" and I always wonder what the view matters as I sit in the corner of the room reading Wordsworth, looking for a quote to put in this book.

> *Our birth is but a sleep and a forgetting.*
> *Not in entire forgetfulness,*
> *and not in utter nakedness,*
> *but trailing clouds of glory do we come.*

Love to M, Steve.

April 27, 2011 – New York, NY

Steve,

As a frequent traveler, you no doubt welcome good travel tips. I am now going to offer a bit of travel advice for which you will be thanking me for years to come. This is hard-won knowledge I am passing on, but I give it to you gratis.

You are no doubt aware of a strategy which has been used with great success in a number of different fields and is usually called "contrarian." If the entire financial community is pouring money into high-flying tech stocks, the contrarian investor starts buying dull public utilities or maybe even sells tech stocks short.

In the film industry, if an actor has made his career playing big, manly lady-charmers, the wily contrarian director casts him "against type" as a gay rent boy. A year later both the director and the actor have Oscars on their mantels.

When every major league baseball team is engaged in bidding wars over power-hitting, home run men, the contrarian general manager is building his team on speedy, singles-hitting, fielding wizards at pennies on the dollar.

Now here's the tip: when you're in a strange city and selecting a restaurant – do *not* be a contrarian. Go with the flow.

For instance, in a few weeks I will be in Italy for 30 days. During that time I will have 30 Italian dinners. I will not make the mistake of one night saying – hey, Miranda, how do you feel about a Mexican dinner tonight? … Or, let's go out for some sushi.

I have been in Italy for maybe 30-35 days of my life. I've spent time in Rome, Venice, Naples, the Amalfi Coast, Florence, Tuscany and Sicily. In all that time in all those places I've *never* had a bad meal. Which is not to say that all Italian meals are great; the worst Italian meal I've ever had was in Paris. The worst Mexican meal I've ever had – I mean it was pretty much inedible – was in Moscow. The worst paella I've ever had was in Oslo. The worse Chinese meal I've ever had was in Mexico.

To boil this advice down to a simple, easy-to-remember phrase that I just came up with, I'd say: When in Rome do as the Romans do. I give you permission to quote me, but when you do you must always give me credit as the originator of the phrase.

Going to Maine soon? Go to a clam chowder and lobster place. Paris? Go to a bistro and order steak frites. London? Go to Paris.

t.

28 April 2011 – Sun Valley, Idaho

Hey, Terry,

I feel like I'm in a scene from *The English Patient* as our small plane flies between mountains into the tiny patch of landing strip in Ketchum, Idaho. Was I scared? Well, yeah.

When I got to my hotel in Ketchum I pulled your postcard out – the one I got over a week ago, with the picture of the snow-covered library you go to in Canada to use their computers for your emails. Libraries are part of our past. I remember the one in Birmingham, Michigan, you and I would go to so you could do research on Jesse James. That one had patches of snow on it, too. There's a longing there for the old world of silence. For the old world of books.

I decide to walk the streets of Ketchum before the sun goes down. I see a big banner over the street that says "Ernest Hemingway Days Celebration!" – I realize that Hemingway lived here in his last days on earth. Amazing how a writer's name and fame lives on if there's enough power in his work.

Just the other night watching *The Croupier* (great movie, second viewing) with Kathy, the Clive Owen character quotes Hemingway at a crucial moment, "Sometimes, when a man is broken, he becomes stronger in the broken parts." I am in Idaho to do some consulting.

They say that Hemingway loved the sports and woods of Ketchum and Sun Valley, and the terrain of Idaho reminded him of terrain he knew and loved from areas around the world. Hemingway would use the mornings as his time to work. He would write until about 11:30, and then go hunting with his friends. His body is there today alongside his wife Mary and granddaughter Margaux who committed suicide in Santa Monica years later. Some of Hemingway's greatest works were written while he was in Idaho. In the fall of 1939, Hemingway finished *For Whom the Bell Tolls* right here where I'm walking around. It was written in Suite 206 of the Sun Valley Lodge where I did my seminar. He also had a temporary bar and bookshelf installed just for him, at the Sun Valley Lodge. At Trail Creek Campground, you can hear water rushing over rocks while you look at that grave site. The whole of beautiful Idaho is here where Hemingway lived, wrote and died.

I love how you love Paris. Because you are traveling all over you probably will not have a chance to see *Midnight in Paris* ... the new Woody Allen movie. I know you are not a great fan of his, but this one you will like I am sure. (Movies, for me, are a great way to travel without having to go through customs.)

S

5 May 2011 - Myrtle Beach, South Carolina

Dear Terry,

On the plane from Phoenix to Atlanta, where I would change for a flight to Myrtle Beach, I read the book you sent me, (*Life Work* by Donald Hall.)

I underlined something the famous sculptor Henry Moore said to Donald Hall in the book. Hall had asked Moore – now that Henry Moore had just turned 80 – what Moore thought the secret of life was.

Moore said, "The secret of life is to have a task, something you devote your entire life to, something you bring everything to, every minute of the day for your whole life. And the most important thing is – it must be something you cannot possibly do!"

Moore's task was to be the greatest sculptor who ever lived and to know it.

Most people would think that was a bit obsessive. Most people would scoff at that kind of ego. But I must be different than most people, because when I read that quote I was lit up for hours after! I loved it! Because when I read something like that I know that that's what I want to do with my life, too.

I'm not going to say what my task is, because boasting about it or predicting it takes energy away from the actual doing of it. Which I am in the process of even as we write to each other!

Do I care to share my strategic plan to achieve this impossible task? Not at all! (I used to do things like that. And the energy it took to conceive of a grand plan and then brag about it would rob me of the energy necessary for the execution of the plan. So. No more.) I like what Southwest Airlines' brilliant boss Herb Kelleher used to say: "We have a 'strategic plan.' It's called 'doing things.'"

I'm here in Myrtle Beach, South Carolina, to help a friend and client.

Myrtle Beach is known for many things ... It sports titles such as "The Seaside Golf Capital of the World," "Branson by the Sea" [*editor's note: Branson, Missouri, nestled in the Ozark Mountains, is known as a music Mecca. Especially country music. In a town of 10,000 inhabitants there are more than 50 live performance theaters. TNH.*] "The Campground Capital of the World," and "The Miniature Golf Capital of the World." It has been called the "Hottest New Destination" by *Destinations Magazine* in 1994, and one of "10 Outstanding Family RV Vacation Destinations," by the Recreational Vehicle Industry Association in 1995.

And as my driver took me from the airport to my hotel I was entranced by the lush greenery, the waterways everywhere, and the beautiful old homes. I was immediately reminded of Emerson's essay called Compensation. In it he notes that every place on earth, no matter how beautiful, has a compensating downside to it. And vice versa: no matter the downside, there's a hidden beauty.

I could see the beauty in Myrtle Beach (especially since I'm fresh from a hot desert spring). But what would the downside be? As I peered out the window I wondered, then it hit me. Lush, tropical greenery? Reptiles!

"Do you have snakes here?" I asked the driver.

"Oh yeah. And they're not fun."

"What do you mean?"

"Well, I'm from upstate New York where you had snakes but they were harmless, garden snakes. Here they're poisonous."

"Poisonous?"

"Yup. Do you golf?"

"Not much. Not since 1958 actually."

The driver said nothing.

I said, "Why do you ask?"

"Well, there's about 40 golf courses here within a 100 mile radius. And when you hit a ball in the rough? Better just play another ball."

"Because of the snakes in the rough?"

"Right. And it's not just snakes."

"Not just snakes?"

"No. There are alligators on the golf courses too."

"Now you're kidding."

"Nope. You'll come up on a hole and they'll be right there sunning themselves by the water hazard."

We drove in silence for a while, as I thought about the word "hazard." You could think of the poisonous snakes and the alligators as hazards, too. Like in miniature golf, where the hazards often move. Moving, reptilian, poisonous hazards.

My hotel overlooked the ocean, and the waves rolled in all night. The strange combination of rolling sand dunes and giant oaks looming over wide sandy beaches make Myrtle Beach unforgettably beautiful. I couldn't get the Gram Parsons song out of my head, *Hickory Wind*. "In South Carolina, there are many tall pines, I remember the oak tree, we used to climb." I finally could see what the grievous angel was singing about.

The town's name, "Myrtle Beach," is in honor of the Sweet Myrtle Tree, a waxy shrub native to the area. I was here two days, the highlight of which was going to the Carolina Opry and seeing their amazing cast (including Calvin Gilmore) put on a musical show as good as anything I've seen in Vegas or New York. I hope to return to Myrtle Beach many times.

Will I play golf? I'm not a great animal guy, so I'd say no.

Steve

15 May 2011 - Gilbert, Arizona

Terry,

It was great talking to you on the phone and catching you in NYC right before you are leaving again, this time for Europe. I was sorry to hear about the Off Track Betting being closed in NYC thereby slamming the door on our tradition of placing Kentucky Derby bets with you. I would have bet on Animal Kingdom. I'm almost sure of that.

You told me on the phone that you'd received your copy of my latest book, *Time Warrior.* I confessed that my basing the entire book on a quote by Bruce Lee was an attempt by me to get Miranda to read one of my books. I know she reads the ones that you are co-author of, because they are obviously smart and witty ... the kind of book an artistic New Yorker like Miranda loves to read.

But my other books, the non-fiction self-help stuff, are not the kinds of things she normally goes for. And even you (who, as a loyal friend, have read all my books thank you) are not a great fan of self discovery as we have learned in these very pages.

So to see if I might captivate Miranda I have based the entire *Time Warrior* book on a quote by Bruce Lee. You'll see that quote at the very beginning of the book, "The successful warrior is the average person with laser-like focus." I know that Miranda is of Chinese heritage, and that her last name is Lee. Therefore she is most likely *related* to Bruce Lee which gives me added pop in this bid for her readership. Notice that on the cover of the book, the warrior could be a woman, like Xena was a warrior. Many times throughout the book I use the pronoun "she" to refer to what a time warrior would do in a certain situation. A concession to gender equality? No, quite obviously, an attempt to see if I can get Miranda to keep reading once she starts.

Now, I don't know if you two listen to the radio in New York. I know you don't drive around Manhattan in a car, so there's no car radio in your life, so you probably missed the interview I recently gave on the occasion of the release of this book. I include a partial transcript, my answers in CAPS:

(Show host:) You say *Time Warrior* is violent, do you mean really violent?

YES.

Why violent?

BECAUSE VIOLENCE IS MISSING. PEOPLE DON'T HAVE TIME MANAGEMENT PROBLEMS. THEY HAVE COURAGE PROBLEMS.

How so?

THEY ARE AFRAID TO SAY NO. PEOPLE ARE AFRAID TO SAY NO. YOU YOURSELF INCLUDED. TRY IT. YOU'LL SEE. TRY TO SAY NO. YOU SIMPLY CAN'T. THAT'S WHY I WROTE THE BOOK. SO PEOPLE COULD SEE THAT.

What have people said about the book so far?

I ASK PEOPLE IF THEY LIKE IT, AND DO YOU KNOW WHAT THEY SAY?

What do they say?

THEY SAY NO!!!!!!

So the book must be effective.

YES. VERY.

    S.

18 May 2011 – Barcelona, Catalonia, Spain

Steve,

Our flight from New York arrived here at about 10:15 in the morning. By noon we were in the apartment where we'll be staying for the next month.

It's the apartment of our friends Jordi and Steffi who will remove themselves during our stay here to a second apartment they have in Munich. This place has two beautiful sunny studios that front on the broad boulevard Passeig de Sant Joan. From the front balcony, on the right, you look to the mountains that back the city; to the left, down to the Old Town and the Mediterranean Sea, just visible about two miles away.

We're on the edge of a wonderful neighborhood called the Gracia. Ten years ago it was considered up-and-coming, but now, Jordi tells me, it's probably the second most expensive real estate area in the city. I guess it's already come.

After unpacking, Miranda and I walk the neighborhood. Having stayed in this apartment several times before for a total of almost half a year, we know the area quite well. Little has changed (except the real estate prices I suppose) from our first stay here back in the spring of 2004. It still feels vibrant.

The Gracia is dotted with seven or eight small squares, which are always full of life. In this Mediterranean climate, the outdoor cafes are used virtually year round, crowded with artists, writers, designers, architects, editors, students, film makers and young professionals. Across Europe this real-estate-inflating class are known as bo-bos, bourgeois-bohemians.

Steffi and Jordi would certainly qualify. She's a novelist, television and film writer and speaks six languages that I know of; Jordi is a novelist, memoirist, journalist who writes two weekly columns for

El Periodico, a major newspaper here. On Wednesdays – that would be today – he does a regular 10-minute segment on a radio show. He is also multi-lingual, though compared with Steffi, he seems almost uneducated, speaking a mere three languages. In many ways they are "the new Europeans" so much talked about when the European Union was formed in the early '90s – steeped in their own cultures (Catalan for Jordi; German for Steffi) but pretty much at home living and working anywhere in Europe.

The subject of Jordi's columns and radio segment is, well ... pretty much anything he feels like talking about. This evening on the radio he does a humorous piece on the possibility of Barcelona's sinking into the sea under the weight of the record number of tourists coming to town this weekend.

We meet him afterward at a café in Plaza Virreina in the Gracia. He tells us his radio segment went well. Not being Catalan speakers, we hadn't listened to it. And then, because Jordi will be leaving early tomorrow, we pump him for local color – restaurants, events, sights and bars that will need our attention during our stay.

The dominating event over the next few weeks in Barcelona will actually take place in London at Wembly Stadium on May 28th when Barcelona takes on Manchester United for the team championship of Europe. This is the soccer equivalent of the SuperBowl here on the continent. But for Barcelona it means even more than that.

Even on the ride in the taxi in from the airport the game's super importance is evident if you know what to look for. As you pass apartment buildings coming into the city you see many large banners displayed across the fronts of balconies. Some are maroon and blue banners while others are yellow and red. A first impression would be that these people are fans of two different teams, but in fact both are in support of Barcelona.

The maroon and red is the official FCB (Football Club of Barcelona) standard. The red and yellow is the flag of Catalunya.

The government of Spain might describe Catalunya as a province of Spain, but most of the people who live here think of themselves as Catalunyans not Spaniards. Many, in fact, *resent* being a part of Spain and would prefer to be an independent country. This isn't going to happen, but that doesn't change the mindset.

So while for most international soccer fans the World Cup is the biggest event in the sport, in Barcelona the European team championship is more important. In their minds, Spain doesn't truly represent them in international soccer even though a number of the best players on the team are Catalan. Obviously Catalunya, not being an official country, doesn't have a national team.

Instead, Catalunyans have come to think of Barcelona as their "national" team. This is despite the fact that most of the team isn't Catalan. Some of them aren't even Spanish. For instance, their best player (and, in fact, the best player in the world right now), Lionel Messi, is Argentinean.

A couple of incidents might give you a sense of the ambivalence Catalunyans feel about their nationality and their futbol loyalties:

A few years ago we were living in Barcelona when Spain was playing Portugal in a big international tournament. We watched on television as Portugal beat Spain and eliminated them from the tournament. The next day, walking around the neighborhood I saw a piece of fresh graffiti on a wall in one of the Gracia squares. It said: "Thank You, Portugal!"

Spain, as you may recall, won the last World Cup in 2010. This produced mixed feelings here in Barcelona, and for many Catalunyans the only thing that made it a good outcome is that Spain's winning goals in the final two games of the tournament were scored by Barcelona players.

Much of this equivocal feeling about Spain goes back to the Spanish Civil War. Barcelona and Catalunya was the Republican stronghold against the Nazi-backed forces of Franco. When Franco won in 1939, thousands of Catalunyans were executed; many thousands more had to emigrate to countries around the world. Many of the political refugees who crossed the border to France were stored in French refugee camps until they were transferred to German concentration camps when the France surrendered to the Germany in 1940.

The Catalans that stayed in Barcelona basically lived in an occupied country for the better part of four decades during Franco's reign. During that time the Catalan language was outlawed in the schools and only Spanish was taught. It wasn't until Franco died in 1975, that Catalunya began to have some autonomy again. All these years after Franco's death, things are obviously much better for Catalunya, but the resentment lingers. Throughout those years of virtual subjugation and since, the Barcelona football team has been a source of pride. And over the years there have been memorable games and season rivalries against the hated Real Madrid team, which is still sometimes referred to as "Franco's team."

In the last six years, Barcelona has made it to the finals of the Champions League three times. Winning in 2006 over Arsenal; in 2009 over Manchester United; and in ten days they'll again face Man U and try to win another Cup. Catalunya is going wild!

t.

20 May 2011 - Santa Monica, California

Terry,

It's great that you've become an international sports fan. You even helped me understand the World Cup last year as I have not progressed like you have to the embracing of soccer as a real sport. I am the Ugly American, thinking any sport that forbids the use of one's arms cannot be a great sport.

Your history lesson on Franco was good ... and it reminded me of a song I learned years ago called *Viva La Quince Brigada*! It's about fighting fascism and Franco. One of the things I loved about the folk song craze in the 1950s is that it opened up Eisenhower's repressed plastic America to a whole new dimension of other countries and other cultures ... the same thing you and Miranda do in your travels.

I am in Santa Monica to deliver seminars, and I love this place. I set my first mystery novel, *The Woman Who Attracted Money,* in Santa Monica so I could give it a kind of written tribute. My talks today were delivered in the charming old Santa Monica Playhouse, and you know quite well how I love being "on stage" especially when it's literal.

And speaking of world travel, the police detective I hired as a consultant to my first crime book is just back from Afghanistan. They embedded him over there for a few months with the American troops to help "detect" the location of various Taliban and Al Qaeda leaders. He is a world-renowned expert on tracking fugitives through their cell phone use, and our "enemy" these days behaves more like a drug cartel or street gang than the old notion of infantry and combat. Therefore the military calls in a top detective to assist them in locating elusive human targets. Brave new world everywhere.

But I am glad he is back, safe and sound, to assist me in my current book, also set right here in Santa Monica. It's called *A Crime of Genius.* Look for it this holiday season in a bookstore near you. Or not. Because bookstores are closing. So perhaps I should have said "Get it on your Kindle or iPad by Christmas!"

Love to M,

S

29 May 2011 – Barcelona, Cataluña

Steve,

Yesterday was the much-anticipated Barcelona versus Manchester United football game I wrote you about several days ago. It was for the team championship of Europe. I've already told you how important this team is to Barcelona so you can imagine how fun it is being here.

The game was in the evening and by game time I doubt there was a soul walking any street in Barcelona. Everyone was perched in front of a screen somewhere. We were in our apartment watching with Miranda's cousin who is here visiting from New York.

The apartment opens in back on a huge courtyard which is surrounded on four sides by apartment buildings. There must be 200 to 250 individual apartments that back on this courtyard and as the game was about to start, I could see television screens in many of these apartments tuned to the game.

It was actually broadcast on two channels. We were watching on the Spanish channel because we at least speak that language *un poco*, but it was also being shown on a Catalan channel. What we did not realize until the first goal by Barcelona at the 27-minute mark in the game was that there was a 3-second delay between the Spanish and the Catalan channels.

It was very funny. We were cheering and jumping around and then *three seconds later* the entire courtyard erupted in a roar. People were at their back windows and on their terraces banging pans and yelling their heads off. Obviously everyone but us was watching the Catalan channel. The final score was 3–1 for Barcelona and we saw each play and each goal three seconds before our neighbors.

After the game we went up to the roof and watched as fireworks went off all over the city in celebration.

I know we sometimes get negative comments on our tendency to write about sports too much in these books, but I want to say a bit about the game itself. It was remarkable, not only a victory over the second best team in football, but absolute domination. Lionel Messi, who is clearly the best player in the world right now, created one goal and scored another. I've never seen anything like it, Steve.

Barcelona controlled the ball 69% of the time, making 777 passes to Man U's 357. They had 12 shots on goal to 1 for the English team. And they did it all on English soil – at Wembly Stadium in London.

Manchester's coach, Sir Alex Ferguson, has been coaching for close to 40 years now and has won well over 2000 games. He said Barcelona was the best team he's faced in all the years he's been coaching. "They mesmerize you with their passing, and we never really did control Messi … but many teams have said that," he said in the postgame interview.

Miranda's parents are visiting for the week and staying at a hotel downtown here. A big parade has been organized for the team which flew home from England last night and Miranda noticed in the paper this morning that the route went right by her parents' hotel. And their room has a view overlooking the street.

So we took the subway down to the hotel, weaved our way through the waiting spectators on both sides of the road and went to their room. The open-topped bus passed right below us, close enough that we could recognize all the players – Messi, Xavi, Villa, Puyol … names that probably mean nothing to you, but they're all household names in this city.

And then, because we were with Miranda's family, we all went out for a great dinner of tapas. No event takes place in a Chinese family without a meal. Then, a month on, while the actual event will be a hazy memory, all the dishes of the meal will still be vivid in their minds. It's a genetic mindset.

From the home of the European Champions,

t.

1 June 11 – Columbus, Ohio

Dear Terry,

I hope you will like the postcard I just mailed you from here. It's a picture of the Ohio State University football field, knowing your passionate devotion to the arch-rival Wolverines of Michigan. I am a great believer that writers like you benefit from jolts … tiny shocks to the system that pull you out of your slumber … ("What's this?!?! A card from the enemy!")

I'm here in Columbus working with 30 directors of nursing from nursing homes in Ohio. The owners of these homes are young, progressive guys who have created wonderful environments for their nursing home residents throughout Ohio. I'm working with the nurses to instill leadership and communication strategies throughout the system.

But here's the coincidence: Kathy reports that you've just sent us an article from the *New York Times* on people who coach the dying. We had joked a couple weeks ago on the phone about my retiring from being a life coach to becoming a Death Coach. As a natural progression. But although I was joking, this article shows that there are such folks already at work. So I've got to look further. I have to break new ground. Maybe I can be a Hereafter Coach. Getting people ready for the afterlife so that they don't embarrass themselves when they get there.

Columbus is a beautiful town, especially when contrasted to the 100-degree Phoenix desert heat in May. Here in Columbus there are beautiful deep green trees and lawns and red and grey Ohio State gear everywhere.

Okay, I'll grant you Ann Arbor is an even prettier college town. You and I used to go hang out there as youngsters, just to take it all in. But Columbus has the advantage of having been written about by Phillip Roth in *Goodbye, Columbus.* One of my previous letters to you was from Newark, and in *Goodbye, Columbus,* Roth's hero is Neil, a poor Jewish boy from Newark. Synchronicity.

On the airplane from Newark to Phoenix I read a book that I bought when I was last in New York, Steven Johnson's *Everything Bad is Good for You.* It's a wonderful book that explains why people are getting brighter and more intellectually powerful every day because of (not in spite of) our pop culture of computer games, video games, reality shows and movies like *Memento.*

He devoted a lot of pages to what he considered to be the forerunner of high-IQ games, APBA Baseball! A game you and I played a lot as kids, so it was great to get confirmation that the very playing of that game boosted our IQs into the stratosphere ... and speaking of "strato" he also saluted "Stratomatic" baseball, which you and I also played, but I never thought was a very smart game, especially compared to APBA. Remember? You'd put those circular cardboard disks on a dial and spin for each player's at bat? APBA was vastly superior and more complex.

Think how dumb we'd be if we hadn't played it ... was Johnson's point. Steve.

POSTCARD FROM STEVE: PICTURE OF SELLOUT CROWD AT OHIO STADIUM IN COLUMBUS. THE OHIO STATE BAND IS ON THE FIELD PERFORMING THEIR SIGNATURE DRILL "SCRIPT OHIO."

(Editor's comment: In the printed section on the back, we discover that Ohio State has received a trademark for the words "The Best

Damn Band in the Land." Which is at times shortened to TBDBITL –
really! And how can they trademark that when the Rolling Stones are
still around? TNH)

Dear Terry and Miranda.

I am here in Columbus giving a seminar and taking in the beauty
of your rival city.

s.

3 June 2011 - London, England

Terry,

Amazing. I am in London! This is the first time I have been here
since 1969!

It's enchanting to see all the greenery and the apartment buildings
and all the scenes so familiar to me from watching my favorite British
TV shows, *Poirot, Hustle, Foyle's War, Morse*, etc. But now it's live.

I am here to give a two day seminar at the lovely old Russell Hotel.
There isn't any time to really go sightseeing, but I do a lot of long
walks around the hotel and take in the neighborhood.

One challenge to me was finding out that the British do not believe
in three holes. I had shipped over 50 workshop binders for our students
to take notes in, etc. and these binders contain standard three-hole
punch paper. But in England there is no such thing. They have two-
hole paper and that's it. It took awhile to solve that problem.

Another thing I noticed. We had two microphones to hand out to
audience members when they had questions for my partner Rich and
me. It turned out that only the British needed these microphones. The
Americans in our course spoke with loud, confident voices. (When
you and I were about 11 years old we made up a word called "blant"...
do you remember? It signified a kind of combination of fulsome and

blatant and obnoxious in voice tone). Americans were blant. The British, however, were so reserved and softspokenly eloquent that their voices needed electronic amplification. Interesting. I had always wondered, in the past, why on the McCartney Unplugged and Clapton Unplugged albums you can't hear the vocals. Now I know. Never unplug an Englishman!

S.

4 June 11 – Barcelona.

Steve.

This is just to tell you that when you were at the Russell Hotel, you were just a few blocks from my office in London where I worked 1997–1999. We were on Bloomsbury Way, next to Bloomsbury Square and just two blocks from the British Museum. You probably walked past the office on one of your walks.

Behind the office was a little enclosed square with various upscale little shops. One of them sold all manner of Bloomsbury Group items. They had books, of course, new editions and antique, written by members of the group (some even signed), plus letters, paintings and drawings, etc. I loved looking around that little store and would often go there during my lunch hour. I'd buy books there and once I bought a small pencil drawing of a woman at a café espied by Vanessa Bell. She signed it "VB." I paid, I think, 500 pounds for it, which at the time was about $750. I have it now in our bedroom here in New York and, I must say, I'm awfully happy with it.

Vanessa Bell is quite a well-known painter in England whereas here she is known primarily, if at all, as the sister of Virginia Woolf. Though three years older than Virginia, she outlived her by 20 years, dying at 81 when we were juniors in high school. Of course, Virginia was at a disadvantage because suicide tends to cut into your life expectancy. In the movie *The Hours*, Vanessa was played by Miranda Richardson to Nicole Kidman's Virginia.

The last time I was in London I saw that the little Bloomsbury shop had closed. I was sorry to see it gone.

t.

6 June 2011 - Gilbert, Arizona

Terry,

Thanks for your London memories … I did remember that you had worked and lived there a few years.

Two things about Virginia Woolf's suicide have always intrigued me. The first is that they say she drowned herself in a river by filling her coat pockets with stones. I've always had a hard time picturing that. What stones would be heavy enough to fit in a coat pocket and pull a human body down below the surface of a river? She was a very poetic novelist, so maybe the stones were symbolic. Maybe they represented the weight of her thoughts. But then why do historians keep saying it was the cause of her death? Those stones???

I am certain that at Dignitas, the assisted suicide center in Switzerland, they don't say, "We have two choices for you, you can do our nice phenobarbital cocktail, which induces a peaceful coma and then death, or we can do rocks-in-the-pocket in the river."

The second thing about her suicide I've always been fascinated by is her suicide note. I think it is the kindest, most heartbreakingly generous note ever written. It was written to her husband and it said:

"Dearest, I feel certain that I am going mad again. I feel we can't go through another of those terrible times. And I shan't recover this time. I begin to hear voices, and I can't concentrate. So I am doing what seems the best thing to do. You have given me the greatest possible happiness. You have been in every way all that anyone could be. I don't think two people could have been happier 'til this terrible disease came. I can't fight any longer. I know that I am spoiling your life, that without me you could work. And you will I know. You see I can't even write this properly. I can't read. What I want to say is I owe all the happiness of my life to you. You have been entirely patient with me and incredibly good. I want to say that – everybody knows it. If anybody could have saved me it would have been you. Everything has gone from me but the certainty of your goodness. I can't go on spoiling your life any longer. I don't think two people could have been happier than we have been. V."

Amazingly beautiful, no?

Thanks for supporting her sister's work.

S.

June 7, 2011 – Barcelona, Cataluña

Steve,

I went yesterday to the Picasso Museum here. And though I was there the minute it opened, there was already a long line for tickets and so I skipped it. I went instead to a café in a square about six blocks toward the sea from the museum. It's a square Miranda and I love and I spent the morning there drinking coffee and reading. That's the great thing about staying in a place for a time; if you miss something today, well, you can always see it tomorrow.

The museum is in an old part of town called the Ribera. It's housed in five now-connected townhouses or palaces built between 1200 and 1400, and the buildings are almost as interesting as the collection. This morning I was at the museum, but 20 minutes earlier than I was yesterday, and I was maybe tenth in line. With a book to read while I waited, this is quite acceptable.

I've been to this museum at least a half dozen times in the last ten years or so, so I pretty much know what I want to see. In terms of quality, the collection is sometimes knocked by critics and it's true that it doesn't measure up to other Picasso collections I've seen (by far the best overall is at the Picasso Museum in Paris), but I love the Barcelona collection. It highlights his formative years and the artist's personal relationship with the city. He loved Barcelona, and it is surely, after Paris, the city most associated with him.

He moved here (after having spent his early childhood in Andalusia and a few years in Galicia) when he was 13 and it was during the next decade while living here that he really became an artist. Here he went to art school and did his early paintings while hanging out with a very avant-garde crowd of artists, writers and Catalan activists in various studios, bars and cafes in the old part of the city.

He moved to Paris, at that time the very center of the art world, in his early twenties, but he never stopped loving Barcelona. He often said, especially as he became like us and wallowed in the drug of nostalgia, that he regarded this city as his true home. And for thirty years after he left, he frequently came here for long stays. It's hard not to love this city.

When Franco took over Spain in the late '30s, Picasso vowed never to return to his country until the man was no longer in power. So for the final 35 years of his life he never once set foot in the country of his birth. It reminds me of Miriam Makeba's 30-year exile from South Africa, though of course hers was on the orders of the South African white government while Picasso's was self-imposed.

The other difference is that when Mandela was released from prison, he asked Miriam to return and she did. Unfortunately Picasso died two years before Franco.

Picasso's lifetime best friend was Jaume Sabartes. They met at the famous Barcelona café El Quatre Gats when they were both about 17. Sabartes was a young Catalan poet of some note and Picasso did a small watercolor of him the year they met. This picture (along with other sketches of El Quatre Gats artists and writers) is in the museum here.

The very next day we took a flight to Rome to start our honeymoon. We had a wonderful and fondly remembered trip. And ever since then as we've lived in various countries for extended periods Miranda has pushed for a return to Italy. I have resisted.

Not because I don't enjoy the country – because I very much do. In fact we've been back to Italy a number of times since our honeymoon – to Venice, Naples, the Amalfi Coast and all over Sicily – but always for a period of only a few days or a week.

No, my objection to Italy comes from the fact that it's a whole new language to learn. If I'm going to be in a place for more than a few days I want to be able to speak the language a bit. And, hey, I'm still just getting the hang of Spanish.

But with an event like a twentieth anniversary coming up, the language thing just didn't hold up as an excuse anymore. So I had to bite the bullet and Miranda went out and picked up a six-week book/ CD Italian course that promised that we could "pick up the basics in just 35 minutes a day."

We started the week before we left for Barcelona and then – just to mess with my mind – continued with it through our four weeks in that Catalan and Spanish-speaking city. So right now we're wrapping up the "basics" during our first week in the land of Joe DiMaggio's ancestors. The results have been predictable: Miranda is able to buzz away easily with everyone from our apartment owner's mother to her "supermarket" consortium shopkeepers. While the only sentence that I feel truly comfortable saying is from the very first lesson (this is an actual sentence from the class and I have mastered it): "Ho bisogno di una bella moglia, una Lamborghini e molti soldi."

This means: "I need a beautiful wife, a Lamborghini and a lot of money." I've only had occasion to use this sentence three or four times in casual conversation since I've been here.

terry.

17 June 2011 - Gilbert AZ

Terry,

You already have a beautiful wife and a lot of money, and I think the last thing you'd really want is a Lamborghini, given your love of trains and subways ... so I recommend changing your go-to phrase. Maybe this: "Where can I do some Jello-shots and play Halo 2?"

S.

17 June 2011 – Rome.

Steve,

I don't think you understand money as well as I, Steve. Yes, we have some money, but when it comes to money, "a lot" (*molti*) is always a relative term. On the other hand you're right about the beautiful wife and the ambivalence on the Lamborghini ... but Jello-shots and Halo 2??? Come on!

One of the first things we read in the English language guide book called, cutely, "Rome*ing*" is that in the Campo dei Fiori there is a place called Sloppy Sam's (I'm not sure what the English translation of that would be) which specializes in Jello-shots! And as for Halo 2, how far do you think I am from the Vatican?

Yesterday Miranda and I went to a wonderful neighborhood just south of the Vatican – La Trastevere. In the off-with-the-old-on-with-the-new spirit that gripped Rome after the country of Italy was formed in 1870, much of the city was torn down. These new Italians wanted new, modern buildings to suit a new, modern country. And who wants these crumbling old stone places anyway?

Because Trastevere was across the Tiber and just that much west of the mainstream, it wasn't paid that much attention during the bull-dozing fever. As a result the narrow streets and old buildings survived to this day. The neighborhood saw hard times for a while but is now extremely desirable. ("Chi-chi" the guidebook said, which I was glad of because I'd never known how to spell the word before.) The place is awash with wandering tourists coming to see its old churches and eat at its many sidewalk-tabled restaurants. Which, I must admit, we did.

But the amazing part of Trastevere for us, having searched in vain two days for a tourism office, was the sudden appearance – right there on the main street of the district – of a tourism kiosk!

Inside, we picked up a handful of information brochures and leaflets and then Miranda asked about a race track. The woman behind the counter explained that horse racing was over for the season and that the track was being set up for a world music festival right now. In fact, she said, the last racing day was – and here she checked the internet site – today.

Today!?!

A bus ride, a subway trip, another bus ride and an hour later we were walking through the gates of Ippodromo Roma Campanelle. We got there in time for the fifth race of eight on the card. The track is in the country and quite pretty so it makes for a very pleasant day, even though the racing is not top-rank. The purses were anywhere from $4000 to $12,000, whereas in New York, the *cheapest* race would be worth $30,000. But they run thoroughbreds and they're beautiful and they let you bet on them so I'm here.

After bumbling through a quick language lesson to learn the words for "win" and "place" we placed bets on the fifth race. I then proceed to lose my first three races. But in the last race of the day I bet a couple of euros on a horse named Rubin Hurricane ("at one time he coulda been the champion of the world") at 4–1.

The race was a sprint at 1100 meters (about five and a half furlongs in U.S. terms) with 16 horses and the course was straight like they run quarter horse races. So it all looked something like a cavalry charge. And with all the horses coming at us there was no way I could tell who was in front, but when they got a hundred or so meters from the finish line I could see Rubin Hurricane in the lead and widening.

He paid €10.02 to win so I came out ahead on the day, not counting my two beers. There was no entrance cost because, after the third race they open the entry gates to the public. So you see, Steve, I don't need "*molti soldi*" but I still count it.

You know how I've always loved race tracks and I was very glad to add this one to my collection. I've now been to a total of 27 different race tracks in 7 different countries. My best to Kathy as I'm remembering our day at Saratoga two years ago.

t.

18 June 2011 - Gilbert, AZ

Terry,

You took me back referencing the Bob Dylan song about Rubin Hurricane Carter. Recently *Rolling Stone* magazine listed the 50 best Dylan songs and included some bad, silly songs in the list and LEFT OUT Dylan's best song ever … in my opinion … *Joey*. The song is about the life and death of mobster Joey Gallo, who had been killed on his birthday at Umberto's Clam House in Little Italy.

Umberto's is on the corner of Mulberry and Broome, have you eaten there? It's still open. I know you're in big Italy now, not little. But I thought your memory might serve. Both "Hurricane" and "Joey" were on the same Dylan *Desire* album.

s.

18 June 2011 – Roma, Big Italy

Steve,

I've never eaten at Umberto's, though I keep saying I should. Miranda's eaten there several times before she met me. I assume it was while she was going out with some Family hotshot. She doesn't tell me much about her previous boyfriends, allowing my wild imagination to populate her past love life. Next time you come to New York why don't we have dinner there?

I'd like to go there because that would make two restaurants I've eaten at that have been the scenes of a mob hit. The other was Sparks, on 46th Street, just two blocks from where I used to work in 1985 when, on December 16th, Paul Castellano, then head of the Gambino Family, was assassinated along with his driver coming out of the restaurant. I was not in the vicinity at the time.

The story is that Sparks business really picked up after the incident. The place is very expensive, but I've eaten there several times … when I was on an expense account.

So take your pick, Steve; we can go to either.

t.

19 June 2011 - Gilbert, Arizona

Terry,

I am just back from another Santa Monica trip. Lovely, cool, humid, ocean breezes, great clients, a fun little hotel called the Ambrose where

I stay. It's like a Japanese zen garden made into a hotel.

Now home, I read the postcard and letter you just sent us from Barcelona. It included the Casa Asia Film Week brochure. You wrote that Miranda went to a film there about Bruce Lee and it was awful. That's too bad! Because I think the biopic in America called *Dragon* was wonderful!

But reading the film festival brochure (it's in Spanish, but remember, I learned Spanish in Mexico City, so I can read this thing!) I see that *Bruce Lee My Brother* by Manfred Wong and Raymond Yip is a film that is the first in a proposed trilogy, and that this one focuses only on Bruce Lee's early childhood in China before he even travels to the United States. No wonder. Wong and Yip might as well have called it, *Bruce Lee: The Boring Years*.

You know I love Bruce Lee. He has been my inspiration in so many ways. The American movie about his life was full of joy and energy and therefore caught the essence of who Bruce really was. Will Wong and Yip do that in the remaining two parts of the trilogy? We may never know. Should I call Wong and Yip by their improbable first names, Manfred and Raymond?

Anyway, thanks for the mail. We love all the things you send.

S.

21 June 11 – Rome.

Steve,

We've been here a week now and it's time to record some initial findings:

First, pizza is apparently not round in Rome. It is more rectangular with rounded corners, resembling the shape of the track at Churchill Downs rather than what you'd expect to see when you open a Domino's box. Nor is it served by the slice or cut with a knife. You simply indicate somehow (I use my hands rather than my Italian) how big a piece you want and the person behind the counter cuts it to your specs with a pair of scissors. She then wraps it in paper, weighs it and you're charged by the gram.

Second, there seem to be as many motor-scooters as cars here. As a man whose impressions of Rome were first formed from afar, by watching *Roman Holiday* with Gregory Peck and Audrey Hepburn, and (even more impactfully, strangely) *Rome Adventure* with Troy Donahue and Suzanne Pleshette, the ubiquity of motor-scooters should not surprise me. Both these films feature romantic Vespa scenes that made lasting impressions on me. Still, I suspected they were snapshots from the past, black-and-white visions of the '50s and '60s and as dead today as the four actors who starred in them. (Yes, Steve, even Troy is dead.)

But as I am witness, the scooters live on here. As they never even caught on in New York. Part of this difference from New York is obviously weather. Four to five months out of the year you'd be putting your life at serious risk riding a scooter in New York. But in much-more-temperate Rome, you can think of it as year-round transportation. Another reason, though, is economic. Not only is a scooter much less expensive to buy than a car, it's also much cheaper to run. Gasoline costs about $7.50 a gallon here and it becomes a factor.

Virtually 100% of the cars in Rome are small – some *very* small. I don't believe I've seen a single SUV here. I also don't notice much drug trade. This is in line with the established truth – well-documented in all movies and TV shows that feature drug dealers – that wide-spread SUV ownership causes the drug trade.

t.

June 22, 2011 - Gilbert, AZ

Terry,

No round pizza in Rome? Isn't there a restaurant or something there called the Leaning Tower of Pizza? I think it's famous. Maybe you just haven't looked hard enough.

But I may be revealing myself as an ugly American versus your own Citizen of the World. And I'm happy to live up to that caricature if it makes a better book. I've always marveled at your ability to live in Canada, Paris, London, Mexico, etc. And I mean *live* there, not just visit.

I enjoy your accounts of Italy. Back here in Gilbert, Arizona, the big news today was that we had a dust storm. The skies were a sandy-colored haze as the sun beamed lavender streaks into the sky and the wild wind stirred up little dust devils in the back yard. In a land of no weather and 117-degree heat, a dust storm can be very exciting.

Love, s.

24 June 2011 - Beverly Hills, California

Terry,

We are just settling in now at the Beverly Hilton Hotel where we come June of every year to attend the University of Santa Monica's fundraising dinner called An Evening of Magic.

Each year they have a wonderful, talented magician perform and I am always entertained far more than I expect to be.

As I got in to my seat on the flight over from Phoenix I remembered my flight a few weeks ago to London that began in Phoenix. As we settled in to cruising altitude the pilot came on the intercom and said to us, "Now here's something you don't want to see. Look out the right side of the plane and down below there are forest fires burning … the largest fire in the history of Arizona."

I looked and it was interesting and impressive. But I thought about our pilot's comments. Why would he point out to us something he thought we didn't want to see? Of course we wanted to see it, which is why he pointed it out. He might have meant, "Here's a fire you don't want to be in right now."

And that brings me to something that really annoys me. When people know you are flying, why do they say, "Have a safe flight!" I can understand people saying, when you leave their home, "Drive safely." That makes sense because you have control over your driving, and it's a nice reminder.

But why, "Have a safe flight?" What can I do about having a safe flight? Nothing! So what they are saying is, "I hope you don't crash." But why would they want to say that? Crashes are rare, even though media coverage gives us the impression that they are less rare. But, in fact, they are so rare that you are actually safer in the air than you are on the ground.

Yet people say, "Have a safe flight!" Here's what they mean, "Oh you're flying? I sure hope the plane doesn't catch fire or hit another plane in the sky or get blown up by terrorists or hit some awful weather and lose a wing and have you smashed up and burned beyond recognition. I hope that does *not* happen to you! Not on *this* flight. And I wanted to say that to you because you looked so relaxed about your flight that I thought you might not have been aware that it *could* crash, so I knew if I called out 'Have a safe flight,' it would remind you that it could go horribly wrong. Just in case you were getting complacent about your flight."

I know you face this moronic tendency yourself when it comes to living, as you do, part of the year, in Mexico.

"Oh? Mexico? Wow. Well be safe! Be safe Terry and Miranda, don't get murdered or decapitated by a drug cartel. Or anything like that. We love you."

People project their own idiotic infantile fears on others. It's like walking up to someone and spraying them with a shit mist. But they think they are spraying love and concern. "Be safe! Have a safe flight!"

But they're just offloading their own superstitious poison onto you.

How about just saying, "Have a pleasant flight." Or, "Enjoy your travels!" What could be wrong with that?

Sometimes I feel like interrogating my IQ-challenged well-wisher:

WW: Have a safe flight.
Me: What do you mean by that?
WW: I mean ... well ... I just want you to be safe.
Me: How would I not be safe? What are you referring to?
WW: You know.
Me: Do you know something about this flight that I don't know?
WW: No, no! I just ... well, maybe "safe" isn't the right word.
Me: Why would you use the wrong word? Did you misspeak?
WW: No, I mean, everybody says it.
Me: Oh, okay, you are just trying to say what everyone says? Could you experiment with thinking for yourself?
WW: No. Yes. I just thought it was ...
Me: Here's a suggestion. Why don't you take a long walk on the beach and see if you can figure out what *you* would like to have people say to *you* when you fly.
WW: Right ... because I know when they say "Have a safe flight" I always think of the alternative.
Me: Do you? Me too! I'll be darned.

Anyway, it's time to enjoy California and sitting by the pool. I just hope nothing happens like last year's trip. The whole thing with Leonardo DiCaprio. Did I tell you? I'll tell you about that sometime.

Love to Miranda,
and be safe,
Steve

25 June 2011 - Beverly Hills, California

Terry,

Strange wild night tonight. We dressed up for our evening out, the University of Santa Monica fundraiser, and Kathy looked great in a tie-dye dress and bright blue toenail polish with enough sparkling glitter in it to dazzle any eye. Her toes were like Dorothy's ruby slippers but the color was blue.

I called her "Popsicle Toes" because of the jazzy song I love by Diana Krall with that name.

We went to the evening of magic where psychic-magician Wayne Hoffman wowed the crowd. In the crowd was a girl you and I went to junior high with, Leigh Taylor- Young. She's an actress now.

I think you have claimed to recognize her beauty and destiny way back then, while I missed it … not being a visual person.

Anyway, after the event, we came back to our hotel where they were having some kind of R&B Awards night in the main ballroom. As we walked into the crowd I saw Puff Daddy up close. (P. Diddy, Diddy, Sean Combs … you know who I mean) and he walked right past Kathy and me with his security entourage. He pretended not to recognize me and, hey, I was cool with that.

Then we got onto the elevator and were joined by Paul Williams and his wife. Remember Paul Williams the singer-songwriter who wrote so many hits including *We've Only Just Begun*? He was also on the *Love Boat* and wrote the theme to that memorable show. Paul and his wife were quiet in the elevator and so were we. Until they saw Kathy's toes. Then they both lit up and started praising them. Paul then said, "And the award for best toes tonight goes to …" and Kathy laughed and said, "I gratefully accept …"

I realize now that this whole scenario may make us seem like frivolous, star-gazing people. The world has a lot of trouble and strife in it and here we are in an elevator laughing with a *Love Boat* star about Kathy's popsicle toes. But still! It was yet another incident in the snowballing happy absurdity of my life … the wildly funny moments that I can't seem to stop from happening.

So, therefore, it reminds me of Paris.

I mentioned we saw *Midnight in Paris*, the new Woody Allen movie. And I know you have lived in Paris, you visit there often, and love Paris more than anywhere else. I've not been there yet, but I have always loved Buffy Ste. Marie's *Guess Who I Saw in Paris*. So I will go. I am influenced unduly by music.

But we're talking about absurdly happy moments, right?

So I am reading this book by David McCullough called *The Greater Journey: Americans in Paris*. I highly recommend it.

In it he talks about the American sculptor, Augustus Saint-Gaudens, who moved to Paris to work in more friendly artistic surroundings than America could offer. But soon his life fell apart. His wife left him. His health declined. He had a devastating tumor in his lower intestine. He surrendered to total depression and decided to commit suicide. He went to the Seine river, climbed a high bridge, and was about to end it all, when, as he recalled, "I saw the Louvre in the bright sunlight and suddenly everything was beautiful to me."

Paris saved his life.

Love to M, Steve

29 June 2011 - Gilbert, Arizona

Terry,

I have enjoyed your travel tips this far. Your advice on food, etc. benefits me and every one of our readers. So I thought I'd try to keep up with you by adding one of my own. It's this: breathe.

Often on my travels I forget to breathe. I am doing the tourist thing, or trapped in the hotel, or up in an enclosed aluminum airplane worried about germs, and my breathing gets shallower and shallower as the trip goes on. Soon I'm like a panting puppy, barely getting oxygen. Often I long to get back home where there's plenty of oxygen and the skies are not cloudy all day.

Then I remember what Elizabeth Barrett Browning said: "He lives most life whoever breathes most air." She suffered all her life from lung problems, and finally died after taking way too much morphine to ease the pain of an abscess on her lung. But in her move from England to the open air of Italy, she discovered the life-giving properties of deep breathing. She fell in love with Robert Browning and wrote, "How do I love thee? Let me count the ways."

So my travel tip is to throw open the windows and breathe deeply wherever you land. Walk (as you do) and breathe while you walk. It makes for a much better trip, and it is easily forgotten.

S

ps- I realize that I was being judgmental when I said she ingested "Way too much morphine." Maybe in the final edit I will change that to, "She died when she took just the right amount of morphine."

July 1, 2011 – Rome.

Steve,

I note in some of your recent letters a certain, I'm not sure if "fascination" is the right word, but at least an unhealthy interest in suicide and death (note your speculations on Virginia Woolf, Augustus Saint-Gaudens, Elizabeth Barrett Browning and your thoughts on the phrase, "Have a safe flight.") I sincerely hope that this is simply in the nature of a hobby or a casual pastime rather than a sign of your advancing age or a change to a morbid turn of mind. After all, I am –

as you've often cruelly pointed out to me – almost four months older than you … besides, I'd hate to lose you. Who would I write to?

And while I have no wish to feed into this macabreness, you might be interested in a visit Miranda and I made to the Keats-Shelley House here at the foot of the Spanish Steps. I had to talk Miranda into going with me on the promise of a drink afterwards at a bar/restaurant near the Steps that she's particularly fond of. In general she refuses to accompany me to cemeteries, catacombs and other places of death. Which is what the Keats-Shelley House is. For it was here that Keats died, for the most part unknown, at the age of 25. Tuberculosis.

The "museum" is only four rooms, one of which, very small but with a window looking out on the Spanish Steps, is where Keats spent his final days and breath. The other three rooms have on display many letters, drawings, paintings and ephemera relating to Keats, Shelley and Byron (who gets no play in the naming of the museum.) Many of them very interesting.

Among them are: some letters from Mary Shelley (Percy Bysshe's second wife) who is probably best known as the author of *Frankenstein*; some factually incorrect paintings of the discovery of Shelley's body washed ashore on the Italian Riviera and of his cremation; plus a letter and a drawing of Keats by your friend Elizabeth Barrett Browning who was apparently kind of a Keats groupie. Liz was only 15 when Keats died, but later in life she became a bit obsessed by his poetry and life – to the extent that she corresponded with at least one former acquaintance of his who she pumped for tidbits of information about him. One of these letters with a small line drawing of Keats in profile is here.

Both Keats and Shelley are buried in the south of the city at the Protestant Cemetery which I intend to visit next week without, of course, Miranda. She claims that she gets physically ill in cemeteries and that during our visits I insist on hiding behind trees and headstones and making ghost noises. This last is unfortunately true.

Also buried in this treasure trove of a cemetery, despite his having died in Minnesota somewhere, are the remains of the Beat poet Gregory Corso. Go figure.

Terry.

6 July 2011 - Gilbert, Arizona

Terry,

I know I mentioned dust storms in Arizona a few days ago, but last night was the biggest one we have ever had. It made the national news … so I thought you'd see it on the news last night, but then I realized that you are on Roman holiday, so the storm would have to be big enough to make *international* news for you to see it.

It was huge, with no visibility anywhere! And it was beautiful in a hazy, mysterious way. This morning Kathy and I went into the back yard to pick up some very large branches that had been torn from trees in the storm. They were hard for us to lift and hoist over the adobe wall into our neighbor's yard.

While we were working Kathy marveled at the storm last night and how it shook our windows and rattled our walls. I asked her if she realized that this storm was *all we ever were.*

"What?" she said.

"Last night was all we have ever been."

"What do you mean?"

"Dust in the wind. All we are is dust in the wind."

"Oh, right."

We live in heavy times, don't you agree, Terry? Almost biblical in scope.

[*Editor's note: for those of you not as fascinated by popular song lyrics as Steve, I'll mention that the lines he quotes are from a 1977 song "Dust on the Wind" by the band Kansas. TNH*]

Love – s.

PS- These dust storms are called *haboob*s. *Haboob* is a word from the Arabic meaning ungodly AWESOME dust storm. I remember back in 1962 that you and I went to *Lawrence of Arabia* downtown in

Detroit and you were absolutely mesmerized by the movie. Now I can understand why. First of all, you looked a little like O'Toole in that film, so it gave the adolescent you a kind of physical picture of who you might become. And secondly, Lawrence was a man of the world, loving foreign lands and adventure. Look at you now. You lived into it! Just stay off those motor scooters.

July 7, 2011 – Rome

Dear Steve,

Actually the Phoenix dust storm news got here via the internet, so we were aware and wondering about you guys there. But you're right, it didn't make any of the newspapers. This is a very old city that's seen it all and has been essentially immunized against global-warming-caused phenomena. I mean once you've seen the Visigoths, who can get riled about a silly old *haboob*? Miranda, on the other hand, after seeing the video of the *haboob* that you sent, is pretty much convinced that the world is coming to an end.

Oldness is certainly ever-present here. If you were caught up in antiquities, there would be many places in the city that you'd have on a can't-miss list. The Coliseum, the Forum, the Appian Way, Trajan's Market, etc. Miranda and I saw all of these places when we were here 20 years ago, but not being much of a ruins man, I'm skipping most of them this time.

I am much more interested in the living city and the more recent past; the Rome of today and of Fellini and Suzanne Pleshette and Troy Donahue. Besides, there is no escaping the old here. On a bus ride anywhere in the city you pass buildings, monuments, ancient Roman walls, fountains and sculptures that are many hundreds or even several thousands of years old. But they are not artifacts to be studied; they are physical parts of your life in the city today.

I am right now writing on the edge of the Piazza Popolo, a famous old square with a number of very old churches on it and a beautiful, much photographed by tourists, fountain at its center. One of its churches – Santa Maria del Popolo – has two paintings by Caravaggio just to the left of the altar.

Caravaggio (a contemporary of Shakespeare's, to give you a time reference) was a superb painter, who even today can cause a traffic jam around the Metropolitan Museum in New York when they have an exhibition of his paintings. He was also an awful person, with a fondness for beating people up, trashing apartments he was renting and occasionally killing people. Reading an abbreviated version of his life, I counted five cities that he has to skip out of just to stay a step ahead of Gianni Law.

Talent, of course, has its privileges and he managed to get pardons or get-out-of-jail-free cards for almost all of his transgressions. In fact he was about to beat a murder rap with a papal pardon when he caught a fever and died at the age of 30. This was 1610.

Fast forward 356 years to 1966. Jack Kerouac, at this point deep into the process of drinking and drugging himself to death, is sent to Italy on a book promotion tour. The Italians fail to see him as an important author and instead see him as an out-of-control drunk. All but the then-hot Pop Art artist – Franco Angeli, who picks Kerouac up out of a Rome gutter and invites him to stay at his studio for a few days. During this visit Angeli takes Jack to see the Caravaggios at the Santa Maria del Popolo, just a few steps from where I'm sitting right now.

So impressed are they by the paintings that they return to Angeli's studio determined that they too will do a religious painting. There are a dozen or so religious moments that every serious painter in Christendom attempts at some point in his career: the annunciation, the crucifixion, San Sebastian arrowed, the beheading of John the Baptist, etc. Another mandatory is the "Pieta;" this is a representation of Mary holding, or sometimes just grieving over, the body of Christ when he's brought down from the cross. In English this scene is often called "the lamentation," though "pity" is probably a more exact translation.

Apparently Kerouac had never done a Pieta. (Well, to be frank, Kerouac had probably never attempted any of the great scenes.) Anyway, Kerouac and Angeli decided on the Pieta as their theme and together executed a large painting. This painting then pretty much disappeared for 40 years, though its existence was known.

Well, right now, no doubt in honor of my visit, this very painting is being included in an exhibition here in Rome for the first time and I wanted to see it. The exhibition is primarily of Angeli photographs taken during the years 1966–1975, but it does include a couple of paintings that he did during this period, including his joint effort with Kerouac. As an example of my contention that you simply cannot avoid the Old here in Rome, the show is being held in the Trajan Market Museum. So here you are picking your way around antiquities in this ancient supermarket complex that was built in about 100 AD looking at the art of a 1960s pop artist. It seemed a little weird.

The joint painting itself resembles none of the many Pietas I've seen before. More than anything it resembles what a couple of drunks messing around with paints might create late one night.

We had drinks last evening with a friend of mine who was the head of our Italian office when I was working in Europe ten years ago. When we were leaving the hotel bar he said he was sorry he couldn't drop us anywhere because he drove a scooter. This is a high-level businessman who lives about nine miles north of the city, driving a scooter. Supporting my observation about the number of scooters in Rome, he mentioned that the city was the number-one scooter market in the world.

My best to Kathy,

Terry.

10 July 2011 - Gilbert, AZ

Terry,

I tried to ride a scooter once. It was on a company trip in Bermuda and the company was a client of mine who thought so much of my work that they invited Kathy and me to Bermuda with their top performers.

I hated the scooter. Far from being *Easy Rider*, or Born to Be Wild or Brando in *The Wild One*, I was a tentative, nervous cowardly rider, soaring against my will around winding roads behind big trucks with my idiot helmet on and Kathy on the back yelling for me to man up and go faster.

Now I wonder if when Suzanne Pleshette and Troy Donahue rode scooters in their definitive film about Italy if they had to take a lot of lessons.

By the way, I just got word from my foreign publishing rights agent that a book I co-authored called *100 Ways to Create Wealth* is selling extremely well in Italy. Have you seen it in store windows? However, I read the very same day that Italy is not doing very well financially, so I'm not sure that the book is really working for its readers. It wouldn't be the first disappointing book I've written. A recent reviewer called my most current self-help book "PURE BAFFLEGAB!" and gave it one star out of a possible five. I don't believe zero was an option.

Love to M,

s.

July 11, 2011 – Rome

Steve,

I am writing today from my usual café here. It's not the café you are picturing me sitting in here in Rome, being kind of modern-cafeteria looking, *and* I am indoors, not out on a *terrazza*. To make up for its lack of European picturesqueness, it is air-conditioned, a not inconsequential plus in these weeks, not a day of which has seen the temperature fail to reach 90 degrees.

The café is next to the outdoor concert space, which during June and July is featuring a series of concerts by a lot of big name performers all of whom are probably touring to supplement their monthly social security checks. Even as I write I am actually watching roadies set up for tonight's Ringo Starr concert. At 71, Ringo is not the oldest of the performers; others in the series include: Cyndi Lauper (58), Burt Bacharach (83), John Mayall (77), Manhattan Transfer (the youngest of whom is in his 60s) and John Cougar (who is old enough to have had two careers – one as Cougar and another as John Mellencamp, and whose concert on July 10th I bought tickets for.)

But I interrupt myself. This is supposed to be a letter about how we live here day to day:

Our apartment (small but nicely designed *and* air-conditioned) is on a narrow, quiet cobble-stoned street that allows no cars or scooters. The street is a little longer than the length of a football field with end zones and is lined on both sides with very pretty Italian homes, three and four stories, with wooden shutters on the windows and painted in Mediterranean colors, warm ochres, soft blues and burnt umbers.

In the mornings we have coffee and plan our day. We try not to overdo the sightseeing (after all, we're here for a month) so each day we allow ourselves only one thing – a museum, a site, a new neighborhood walk or an event of some kind. The rest of the day is casual and less structured: shopping, cafes, restaurants, reading, and, of course, writing.

Before the heat gets too brutal, we go for our three-mile exercise walk. From our apartment in one direction it's a 15-minute walk to the huge Piazza Popolo which is in turn the beginning of the Via Corso, probably Rome's main street.

In the other direction, 15 minutes takes us across the Tiber to Rome's Olympic Stadium and facilities. (Built for the 1960 Games, they're getting a bit tattered at the edges now.) We finish our walk each day at a café, usually the small one about ten steps from our apartment.

We eat incredibly well and very differently than in New York or Mexico. Or Barcelona. For instance, in both New York and Mexico Miranda is basically on a low-carb diet. She isn't overly strict about it but if she has a hamburger she'll only eat a quarter of the bun and ration her French fries. Most of the time she lives on salads, vegetables and seafood. Here we live on pastas, breads, and pizzas along with tomatoes, olives, eggplant, Italian hams and cheeses and enough olive oil to lubricate the insides of a large battleship engine. And garlic. Did I mention garlic?

We never found a supermarket, so Miranda works her consortium of a half dozen different markets and shops for the makings of our meals at home, probably about half our total. I don't pretend to be able to follow the intricacies of her complex use of the consortium. She prefers the olives at one shop but the grilled eggplant from another; the server at one market tosses in little occasional extras like special peaches, but another has the particular tomatoes she favors for her salads; water is generic so she'll buy it at the closest shop because it's heavy to carry home, but she doesn't like their white wine, so even though that's also heavy, we get that at a more distant place; etc. Somehow it all gets home, though, and the meals are fantastic!

And we go out each day. Using the elaborate, but not very practical, transit system: interlocking subway, tram and bus routes. There's a tram stop just a short walk from our apartment. And it is the start of all of our trips; it runs frequently and it gets us to Piazza Popolo in minutes at which point we switch to a bus or a subway depending on where we're going.

The subway (the Metro) has only two lines, making a big X under the city. In my experience, none of its stops are anywhere you want to go. Instead the Metro takes you to a place where you can then catch a bus which *will* take you someplace you *are* interested in or, at least, to a place where you can catch another bus or tram aimed in the vicinity of your desired destination.

The number 119 bus is, on paper, the most useful transportation in the city. It goes to virtually every place on our list of must-sees. Unfortunately it never comes. We've been in Rome almost three weeks now and I estimate that two of those weeks have been spent waiting for the 119 – a streetcar named "Godot."

The most notorious bus is the 64, which hits many of the major ancient sites. As a result it's always filled with tourists and pickpockets.

Now's the time for you to start a sandbox,

Love, t.

12 July 2011 - Santa Monica, California

Terry,

I'm in Santa Monica again to do some work with clients here … and, OMG, people can't stop talking about this weekend's upcoming "Carmageddon."

They are going to be shutting down the major freeway in L.A. for a couple of days and they have anticipated gridlock, spillover, and a huge mess.

Amazing how much the west coast depends on cars, while you New Yorkers and many Romans don't even need cars.

For this catastrophic Carmageddon they are going to have all kinds of emergency centers open, and the Metro has offered free rides on 26 bus lines and the light rail system.

Celebrities are getting into the act, too. Because this is California and celebrities tell people here what to do about everything, including who to vote for and what to eat. Most of these celebrities are famous just for being famous. Which is the shallowest kind of accomplishment. Unless you think Erik Estrada and Ashton Kutcher have demonstrated a talent for something. I've never seen that talent.

Yet Erik and Ashton are tweeting and making public service announcements urging motorists to walk during these trying days. Walk! Do you know how spread-out L.A. County is? But, then again, Erik Estrada played motorcycle cop Frank "Ponch" Poncherello on the TV series CHIPS so people are obviously going to go with what he says if it has anything to do with traffic.

There you are in Rome for goodness sake and I am here dealing with this kind of thing. This is the difference between us. You on a culturally rich Roman adventure, and me listening to Erik Estrada telling me what to do about Carmageddon.

Love to M,

s

13 July 2011 – Rome (Miranda's and my 20th wedding anniversary!)

Steve.

Miranda had somehow gotten it into her head that she must see Moses. Not the man himself, but rather Michelangelo's statue of him, housed at the St. Peter in Chains church in the middle of Rome.

Because Miranda was so keen and determined, I did a little research and got more than passingly interested myself.

The statue, completed in 1515, was supposed to be one of more than 40 created as part of a funeral monument for Pope Julius II. The project was never finally realized, but Michelangelo did finish this Moses. Here's the review that the famous art historian Vasari gave it: "No modern work will ever equal it in beauty, no, nor ancient either." Well that got my attention.

After seeing it, I have to say that it's a nice statue ... better than I could have done. So, yes, definitely worth seeing as we approach the 500th anniversary of its creation. Just to give you a perspective, today is the 20th anniversary of Miranda's and my wedding, and that seems like a long time ago right?

But what really captured my fascination at the church was not the Moses, but rather the eponymous "chains" of St. Peter. This is a truly remarkable artifact. And the story that goes with it is not really that well known. It is not as well known as, say, the plot of *Gone with the Wind* or some of the more famous Seinfeld episodes that people are forever retelling, for instance. And it deserves to be. I hope that the next few paragraphs and our wide readership can help begin to right this imbalance:

St. Peter was, of course, a fisherman, who, struck by the preaching of Jesus, left the family business to become a disciple. He was in the inner circle, sort of the cabinet, of Jesus' apostles. One account I read said that he "helped organize the Last Supper." I'm not sure exactly what this means, perhaps he made the reservation or consulted on the menu, but it's doubtful that he baked any bread or stuffed any mushroom caps. Still it'd be nice to have on your resume don't you think? Especially if you wanted to be an events planner.

After Jesus' resurrection, St. Peter continued the work, first around Jerusalem and later here in Rome. And he is generally acclaimed as the first head of the Catholic Church, or the first Pope.

Naturally, if you remember your history or the movie *Ben Hur*, being a Christian back in those early years came with some substantial downsides. One of these was that you had to be prepared to do some jail time. St. Peter did two stretches, one in Jerusalem and a second one later in Mamertine Prison in Rome. The second stint ended badly when he was executed by Nero on Vatican Hill in 64. Famously he was crucified upside down at his request because he felt himself unworthy to die in the same manner as his Lord. Later St. Peter's Basilica was built in the Vatican over his grave.

It is, however, the story of the first imprisonment that is really remarkable. You can check me out on this because it's all written down in the Acts of the Apostles in the Bible. Saint Peter was thrown in prison in Jerusalem by King Herod and kept in chains. The night before his trial, however, an angel came to him, told him to put on his cloak and sandals and follow. At that moment St. Peter's chains miraculously fell away from him and he simply walked out of the prison to freedom.

But here's the real miracle, I think: Over the next four hundred years somebody kept track of those chains and sometime around 440, the chains were presented to Pope Leo I as a gift. (Pretty nice gift, huh?) Leo remembered, or someone reminded him, that right there in Rome they had the actual chains that St. Peter had worn when he'd been imprisoned the *second* time under Nero. Accordingly, Leo got the two sets of chains together to compare them, and guess what? The two chains miraculously fused together! No one could figure it out.

Well, the church Miranda and I went to *has* these fused chains on view every day in a glass box right in front of the altar. Well, okay, that Moses was a terrific statue, but to be able to stand just feet away from the actual chains that not only bound St. Peter, but were also the subject of not just one, but *two*, miracles! Well, I'd say that's worth travelling half way around the world to see.

You know who I believe is really underrated as a thinker and an intellectual, Steve?

P.T. Barnum.

t.

13 July 2011 – Santa Monica, CA

Terry,

I infer from your message that you think P.T. Barnum, known for his phrase, "There is a sucker born every minute," would admire the fused chains on display. Not for their miraculousness, but for the crowds they attract, crowds that include you, sir!

Yet your own credulousness and even, religion, might be more in alignment with that of Annie Savoy in the movie *Bull Durham* who said, "I believe in the Church of Baseball."

How else (but by miracle) to explain the resurrection of my own beloved Arizona Diamondbacks who are playing wonderful baseball this year after some really awful seasons, one of which I heartbreakingly chronicled in our own bestselling *Two Guys Read the Box Scores*?

Why be so skeptical? Are you saying those aren't the actual chains? You were married by an Episcopal priestess (20 years ago today!), very close to Catholic if I know my religion. So are you going to partake *some* infinite spiritual glory but not all? Then again, your discerning brain is also God-given, is it not? So maybe God's pleased that you weren't suckered by the chains. How much did you put in the little coin box, though? That's what I want to know. How much revenue are the chains generating from skeptics like you?

Love to M,

S.

14 July 2011 - Santa Monica, California

Terry,

Still here in Santa Monica seeing clients and enjoying the Ambrose hotel tucked away on a residential side street.

I realized, when I was in London, that you are really a man of the world, especially compared to me. You have lived in London, Mexico, Canada, and Paris, France. Not only that, it seems that every time you touch down overseas you feel a thrill and tell me that you love just being in Europe.

I, on the other hand, am slower to go global. As far as being a citizen of the whole world. When I was in London I did enjoy the quaint charm of it all, and how it reminded me of the great British TV series I have loved, but I was impatient with their slow service. I have been spoiled by a more fast-paced America, and I am almost always traveling in business mode so I am not charmed by bad service as I would be were I just doing a travel adventure.

But I am always ready and willing to learn to be a citizen of the whole earth instead of just "an ugly American."

So I was delighted to notice that my hotel here in Santa Monica was all set up to help me with that. The brochure in my room told me that my Ambrose hotel was dedicated to the entire earth. Not just California. While I was there, I learned that I would be "minimizing the negative environmental impacts" of hotel life and they would introduce me to "a fresh perspective on sustainable living."

My nourishment, they said, would be provided through locally grown and organic foods. My soothing environment would be cleansed, they assured me, with natural, non-toxic products. They said they "prudently borrow the earth's resources through environmental management techniques" and that they would be rewarding me for conservative energy use.

What excited me the most was when I learned, in reading the hotel's brochure, that they have made, for me, "responsible lifestyle choices" without sacrificing my comfort, and that all of this ... when you add it all together ... and this is what lit me up totally ... would be "encouraging thoughtful global citizenship."

Even though this is one small step, I think I am on my way now.

S

July 15, 2011 – En route Rome to New York

Steve.

I'm writing this on the plane back to New York. I wanted to wrap up the Roman month by telling you how we've learned to work the system here in Rome. This is the kind of valuable information that you'd simply not be able to pick up from the casual Coliseum-gawking tourist in Rome (or "Roma," as I, being essentially a native now, prefer to call it). This is serious insider stuff you can only get from someone who has truly lived, as opposed to merely visited, in Rome.

Aperitivi.

This word will drive spell-check crazy. I barely type it and it gets underlined in red. Ignore. In Italy it's the plural of aperitif and basically means "cocktails." But it generally implies something to nibble at too – hors d'oeuvres.

Roman cafes and bars seem to have turned it into something of an institution, the way "tea" is in England, or "happy hour" is in the United States. It is, however, sort of the opposite of our happy hour.

A happy hour will offer drinks at substantially less than the usual price, as in $3 draft beers when they're usually $5, or two drinks for the price of one. In Rome during the aperitivi period, you are asked to pay *more* for your drink. In one place we go, for instance, a glass of wine is usually €6; during aperitivi it's €9. Right now I know you're questioning how attractive an idea this is. But during this period, which usually goes from 7 to 9 in the evening, you are also served platefuls of food: little squares of pizza, canapés, small cups of various pastas, cheeses, cucumber sandwiches, wonderful green olives, brushcetta, etc. All in addition to the usual bowls of peanuts and potato chips.

These are the kinds of cocktails that Miranda can get excited about because it's not really that much about drinking it's all about eating. Some places even set the food up buffet-style and people go over and load up plates. Several times each week since we've been here we've made our evening meal of the aperitivi offerings. I must say we eat wonderfully well here.

Workin' the system.

I caught a glimpse of myself in a shop window I was passing the other day. Do you remember the late Elvis Presley or the late Marlon Brando? By "late" I don't mean "now dead," I'm talking about the later parts of their lives. The body I saw in the window resembled theirs. Put another way – have you seen Jack Nicholson lately?

Mass transit.

I've already told you we basically travel the city on this interconnecting system of subway, trams and buses. Everything seems very expensive to us here in Rome because of the anemic U.S. dollar, but transit costs are an exception. The cost of a ticket here is one euro, or about $1.40. Compare that with a New York subway ride at $2.25 and it seems like a bargain.

To make it even more economical, you only have to know that the ticket's good for 75 minutes. When you get on the tram you go to a little machine and validate your ticket. It prints the time on the back and for the next hour and a quarter you can go anywhere you want on the system. You can change buses a dozen times if you're so inclined, all on the same ticket. Well, naturally, a wise man will tuck that information away and put it to good use when conditions are ripe.

Sometimes in the evening, wanting to go out for a drink, we'll hop the tram down to Piazza Popolo. We find a café or a nice cocktail bar, order our drinks and watch the people and the general activity on the square while the sun sets. Afterwards, I pay the enormous bill (when was the last time you had a$17 beer, Steve?) with a light heart because I know that we're still within 75 minutes of when we first punched our ticket. We'll be riding back on the same ticket that brought us here. Savings: €1 per ticket!

Miranda's new favorite drink is called an Aperol Spritz. A cool, summer-perfect drink consisting of a shot of Aperol (a slightly bitter aperitif) over ice with the rest of the glass filled with prosecco or champagne and a slice of fruit, usually orange or lime. There's a very ritzy hotel rooftop bar just off of Popolo that we found a couple of weeks ago and that we like in the evening. An Aperol Spritz there runs about $30. With my two beers the total bill with tip is about $70. *But* … we know we've saved ourselves €2 on our return tram tickets.

Workin' the system.

Or you can play the whole transit system like a citywide roulette game. This is not for the faint of heart. If you're caught on a tram or bus without a validated ticket, you'll be fined €50. Since tickets are one euro each, you're ahead of the game if they only catch you once in 51 trips.

I will say, however, that since we've been here I've certainly taken more than 50 trips and I haven't been asked once yet to show my ticket. In fact, I've never seen anybody *be* asked.

The Auditorium.

I've already mentioned the concert series held in the outdoor space next to the air-conditioned café I often went to write you. This is the arena with wheelchair access ... for the *performers* they are so aged.

Well, Miranda and I did see John Mellencamp there in a very odd concert. The show opened at the announced start time of 9PM. But it opened with a one-hour-twenty-six-minute film, made by a guy who had *never made a film before*, and his son who had also *never made a film before*. Predictably the footage is very uneven in quality; the sound recording is really very bad, and this is a bit of a drawback in a film that is basically a concert film.

I will grant you that the film is about Mellencamp on tour so that sort of seemed to make some sense. But it also featured a heavy-handed pseudo-philosophical voice over by this guy who'd *never made a film before*. It was as if he were trying to make a super8, badly-recorded film combination of *The Last Waltz* and *Zen and the Art of Motorcycle Maintenance.*

I think I heard the first boos at about the 35-minute mark and they continued sporadically throughout. They did seem most intense when the screen was showing Midwestern landscape shot out the window of a car endlessly blurring by while a voice-over intoned truly sophomoric "deep" thoughts ... *in English* with no subtitles. (Did I tell you we were in Italy where a very large majority of the people speak Italian?)

After the movie, there was about a 15-minute break while the stage was set for the concert we had all come to see. John finally hit the stage at about a quarter to 11 and then proceeded to sing all the same songs we'd just heard him sing in the movie. Although, admittedly, the sound was better.

It is to Mellencamp's credit as a performer that, after basically giving the finger to his audience for an hour and three-quarters, he was able to win them back on stage. He never said a single word to the audience – and didn't give an encore – but he did entertain us with non-stop songs for more than an hour. He did take one break during a long instrumental interlude, sneaking off stage to have a quick cigarette. Or maybe canoodle with Meg Ryan, with whom, according to the Italian tabloids, he seems to be an "item." (Just for the record, Steve, I want to point out that this marks the first time in all my 67 years that I have ever used the word "canoodle" either verbally or in writing. Who says you can't teach an old dog new tricks?)

The tickets for the concert were €55, or about $77. All of the concerts in the series were about the same price, but (and here's the thing the concert producers must have forgotten) ... the Auditorium is *outdoors*. This means that if you're outside the Auditorium at one of several cafes near the entrance, you can hear the concert for free. Or for as little as the cost of an espresso or a glass of wine.

In this way, Miranda and I without buying a ticket heard four or five live concerts, including Cyndi singing "Girls Just Wanna Have Fun" and Ringo doing "Yellow Submarine."

Yes, sir. Workin' the system.

Stick with me for the ins and outs of foreign travel.

Terry.

22 July 2006 – Las Vegas, Nevada.

Terry,

Wow. Yellow Submarine...it's only an hour's flight from Phoenix to Las Vegas, and my client put me up here in this hotel called The Stratosphere. (You will notice that this hotel stationery has a big tower on it. It's like a yellow submarine.)

When I say they put me "up here" I mean "up here." It is a hotel most notable for its tower, which at 1,155 ft is not only the tallest structure in Las Vegas, but also the second-tallest structure in the U.S. west of the Mississippi. (The tallest is the Kennecott Smokestack nearby in Utah. So they say. Whatever that is.)

For some reason, maybe because I was just flat out tired when I got to the hotel, I did *not* take any of the following rides:

The Big Shot at 1,081 feet, the highest thrill ride in the world;

Insanity the Ride, which opened in 2005, and at 900 feet is the second highest thrill ride in the world. It dangles riders over the edge of the tower and then spins in a circular pattern at approximately forty miles per hour. I found out that the ride has stopped twice with passengers onboard (upwards of an hour each time), due to high winds that trigger a "safety mechanism" which shuts down the machine immediately without bringing the passengers back to the loading dock. The hotel is currently being sued by the first set of passengers who were trapped on the ride dangling over the edge;

Nor did I ride **XSCREAM** at 866 feet the *third* highest thrill ride in the world. This ride also "drops" people over the edge, and has also stopped while people were on it, though it is not clear what triggered this ride's failure. Or if the Stratosphere has been served papers on that one yet.

For some strange reason, I just went to bed instead. Resting up for the next day's seminar and coaching sessions with my office product document and copier client. The day's work went well, and on the way to the airport my host, Bob, told me that he was recently on a much smaller Vegas hotel ride with his wife and family and that he had serious problems with his heart and blood pressure even after that mild ride.

Can you tell me, Terry, why people go on these rides at all? Is it just insanity? That answer's too simple.

Now I'm thinking of that lawsuit by the people hanging upside down, up so high, hanging so high for so long. So high you can't get over it: Lawsuit! The only person I ever presented with a lawsuit was a music producer whom we believed borrowed a melody of ours in a song that eventually appeared in the Clint Eastwood movie, *Any Which Way You Can*. That movie also featured the really beautiful Merle Haggard song "Misery and Gin," which I heard performed recently in a steak house by a western band that also played (in the same set) "Carefree Highway" a Gordon Lightfoot hit. Lightfoot wrote the song about the highway near here of that same name as his van was rolling into town to give an Arizona concert. He just pulled out his pen and wrote "Carefree Highway."

When we do the movie of this book, we will want to have that song playing at this point in the film. There will be a great soundtrack album available for this movie, because there are a lot of great songs written about being on the road. Carefree Highway, let me slip away. Slip away on you.

s.

2 August 2011 – Brooklyn, NYC, NY

Dear Terry,

As I was leaving the house ready to board the plane to New York I turned to Kathy and said, "When the cab crosses the Brooklyn Bridge to my hotel in Brooklyn I will, for the first time in many years, be feeling groovy."

Kathy was silent for a moment. Then she said, "'Feelin' Groovy' wasn't about the Brooklyn Bridge."

"It wasn't?" I said, wondering how I'd gotten the old Simon and Garfunkel song wrong.

"No," she said. "It was the 59th Street Bridge Song."

And so I noticed when the car crossed the bridge I was, indeed, not feelin' groovy. But rather in a milder state of enjoyment. I was in Brooklyn to give a seminar on a Friday morning to 564 owners of music and dance studios.

As I woke up that next morning to take my shower before the

seminar I grabbed the tiny plastic bottle of shampoo and as the water pounded down on me I noticed the word "volumizing" on the little bottle. I started washing my hair with it but I couldn't get the word out of my mind. I peered at the bottle again and saw that the letters were actually in capital letters. So it was actually "VOLUMIZING." I decided that it must be a warning. I began to picture myself giving my speech with a HUGE, high-volume head of hair. Hair like boxing promoter Don King used to have. So I cut my shower short and was grateful to see in the mirror that it didn't look like it had any more volume than normal.

The talk went well, and it was fun to walk a bit around Brooklyn and join my friend Sam Beckford (who was hosting the seminar) at a little clam bar to discuss a future book he and I are writing together.

That night I had dinner with Rett Nichols, who used to live down the street on Buckingham Road with us when we were all boys in Michigan. Rett has become one of the top veterinarians in America and gave the graduation keynote address at Michigan State's Vet School this year. We had fun at a VERY nice (jackets required) restaurant called Daniel and vowed to meet again soon in New York and go to a musical together.

I know Norman Mailer lived in Brooklyn Heights, and at dinner at Daniel I reminded Rett of a song he wrote and used to play on his guitar called "Interruption." It was based on Mailer's theory (and the man had many!) that interruption killed the soul and was the plague of modern society ... a theory hatched even prior to cell phones.

While taking a walk in Brooklyn I heard on my headphones Paul Simon's "How Can You Live in the Northeast?" from his new album and I said to myself, "Easy!" It would be fun to live in New York. I wish you had been at your place in New York while I was here and we could have gotten together.

S.

9 August 2011 - Kalamazoo, Michigan

Terry,

Here I am in Kalamazoo to share some seminars with my new clients at Western Michigan University. What a beautiful city of trees and forests and charming houses on hilly roads. And green, green ... like when you are blindfolded, or held captive bound in a closet for a week, and you are set free, and the blindfold is taken off OH the LIGHT floods your eyes.

So too here, does the amazing green of lawns, bushes and trees flood you after so long in the Arizona desert. The people here in Kalamazoo are thinking, What green do you mean? Because they are in it. And it's like Ral Donner tried to teach us, "You Don't Know What You've Got Until You Lose It." I lost it by leaving Michigan for Arizona in my college years. But here it is today in Kalamazoo.

Our parents used to listen to Glenn Miller's version of "I Got A Gal in Kalamazoo" and when Johnny Cash sings "I've Been Everywhere" he proves it by claiming to have been in Kalamazoo. Hoyt Axton said that it was "Della and the Dealer and a dog named Jake, and a cat named Kalamazoo."

So the town's name is very musical. But a strange thing happened. By my third day there I was no longer as impressed by the green. I turned to Kathy and said, "I'm ready to go back to Arizona," as she leaned over to try to hear me over the noise the driving rain was making as it thumped and tumbled onto our rental car. I wanted to go back to where the skies were not cloudy all day.

This is probably why you travel so much. Same reason a pitcher can't live on just a fast ball alone. You gotta have a changeup, a curve, a few more to go to. Otherwise green becomes nothing at all and Samuel Beckett is writing your life story.

S

August 18, 2011 – Detroit, Michigan.

Steve,

A bumper sticker in Detroit from the late '60s used to say: "Will the last person leaving the city please turn out the lights." The exodus from the city had already begun when the riots happened in the summer of 1967, but afterward the pace certainly picked up. Then there was the mass disappearance of jobs when cars started being made in other, often cheaper, places like Europe and Asia and Latin America, but also places like Tennessee and Alabama.

This used to be one of a handful of truly great cities in the United States. Now it's clearly one of the worst. A one-trick pony town without a backup plan.

Neither you nor I will be asked to turn out the lights because we got out … early on. I'm not at all sure that the death of Detroit could have been avoided; but it certainly should have been foreseen. How do I know this? Because I foresaw it. I, who have no training in industrial studies, or economics or city planning; I, who have only open eyes and common sense; I foresaw it. And got out.

Does this sound angry? It should, because I am angry about Detroit. Over 50 years this city has been brought to ashes by the arrogance and stupidity of an industry that believed itself, and its city, to be immortal. When I say "industry," please understand I mean the entire city – the car companies, the unions and the toady politicians.

So here I've been in Detroit for the last three days because, despite what I've just written, there are still some very strong reasons for coming here. As a service to various travel guides and other travel writers, I am listing below the entire list of good reasons for making a trip to Detroit:

It is worth coming to Detroit to have dinner at a very nice restaurant with Mr. Chato Hill and his wife Chris.

It is worth coming to Detroit to spend a long morning over coffee and bagels, telling stories and laughing a lot with Mr. and Mrs. Steve and Shirley Vandenbrook.

It is worth coming to Detroit to enjoy the view of, and a dinner with, Ms. Susan Turner at a very nice restaurant telling stories and laughing a lot.

It is worth coming to Detroit if you have two grandchildren to be able to spend an afternoon with them at the excellent zoo there. It is also worth coming to Detroit to be able to trounce Mr. Ethan and Mr. Cameron Hill at Wii bowling, especially on their home lanes.

It is worth coming to Detroit to go to a Detroit Tiger game with your brother at Comerica Park. Which, to be honest, is a much better place to watch a game than the old Tiger Stadium, despite my fierce emotional attachment to the old place.

If I'd been here at a different time of year I might have tossed in seeing a Lions or Red Wings or Pistons game. But, outside of that, I believe that's pretty much the complete list of possible reasons for visiting Detroit.

But, okay, there is one last reason.

It is also worth coming to Detroit, to pick up your 10-year-old grandson and bring him back to New York for his first ever visit there. This escort service is provided for the fun of spending some time with him and introducing him to the greatest city in the world and perhaps planting in him an ambition that is something beyond being the final light switch thrower.

A wonderful thing I've noticed is that if you write a book (or even in my case, a half a book) about anything, people give you credit for being an expert on that subject. I've had people who know of our Jane Austen book, for instance, come up to me at parties and ask me questions about Jane or one of her books and actually seem to want to hear my opinion.

I find this a strikingly novel thing, anybody caring about what anybody says about anything at a cocktail party.

It's a heady experience: and a humbling one that has made me rededicate myself to my personal mission statement. (I do believe that every person, just like every company should have a mission statement, don't you, Steve? Something trite, but pretentious that you can trot out for people to prove that you, despite all evidence, are a serious human being or at least worthy of holding high public office.)

As you know, my mission is – and has always been – to pass on my accumulated wisdom for the benefit of all mankind, in general, and our readers, in particular.

Essentially, I want to be of service. I want – and you may write this down – to make a difference.

With the publication of this book we will officially become "Travel Experts" and people will start seeking us out for travel advice so I'd like to start the ball rolling right here. On the Detroit to New York flight, I was unexpectedly presented with a very valuable bit of information which I'd now like to pass on as a "travel tip." I believe male travelers especially will find this valuable.

Here it is: If you want to be able to chat up attractive girls on airline flights, you should start by flying with a self-possessed 10-year-old grandson.

When we boarded the plane in Detroit, I sat in the middle of three seats in the second row of the plane, giving my grandson Ethan the window. A pretty, 20ish girl soon arrived to take the aisle seat on the other side of me. She started reading a *Marie-Claire* magazine while I busied myself with the newspaper.

As the plane pulled back from the gate, I heard a voice from the window seat saying, "This is my very first trip to New York; have you ever been before? Hi, my name is Ethan, what's yours?"

Well, after that "Jen" – who was on her second ever trip to New York to visit a male friend for a long weekend (but really they were "just friends," this wasn't a romantic attachment) and who grew up in Ann Arbor though she was currently studying public relations at nearby Ypsilanti because Eastern Michigan University there has a particularly strong department for that sort of thing (i.e. mass communications) (hey, who knew?) and who was currently working as a summer intern at a very highly regarded event-planning firm and after all that was the aspect of public relations that she was particularly interested in – and well, "Jen" just really opened up and the three of us were just like peas in a pod, assuming that one of the peas was a 67-year-old man and one was a 10-year-old boy and one was a pretty, 22-year-old girl from Ann Arbor via Ypsilanti.

This is wisdom I pass on: Obtain a 10-year-old grandson.

Terry.

19 Aug 2011 - Gilbert, Arizona

Terry,

That's quite a powerful group of words you have just assembled and delivered to me.

You and I view the world through different political spyglasses so I won't get into whether your reason for the decline of Detroit is resonant with mine (because a political debate would reduce this book to ashes not unlike the Motor City's.)

But I know you foresaw it, and I did too.

Dorothy Parker's words come forward any time I now get close to Detroit (like recently on my way to Kalamazoo) … "What fresh hell is this?"

And oh, yes, I do relate to our books having given us new and undeserved status at cocktail gatherings.

For example, after you and I wrote *Two Guys Read the Obituaries* people seemed to think I knew something about death itself.

"Where do you think we go when we die?" they'd ask me.

"I don't know."

"Take an educated guess."

"Where does the light go when you turn off the lamp?"

Whenever I don't have answers for people, I go Zen. It can make you sound wise in any situation and save you the necessity of ever educating yourself in traditional, knowledge-based ways, which is tiresome. You do have to read up on Zen, though, which I have done for social reasons.

And Zen recommends that we embrace and even enjoy something called impermanence.

Everything changes.

Even Detroit. And it's good.

Because Detroit is coming back in a new form. Maybe the Lions will make the playoffs this year.

S.

22 August 2011 – New York City

Steve,

Ethan's been staying with us in our New York apartment. As he told Ypsilanti Jen on the plane, it's his first time in the city and I must say it's been fun showing him around and seeing it through his eyes. Reminded me of the first time I came to the City.

(I believe New York deserves that capital C; maybe even a capital T too – The City.)

I was older than Ethan my first time here. I was 15 and the whole family drove from Birmingham, Michigan, to New York in our Pontiac station wagon.

We stayed at the Wellington Hotel on 7th Avenue (it still exists). I remember eating at Luchow's (which is now an NYU dorm on 14th

Street) and also at the Albert Café in the Village (where if you finished a steak at dinner and were still hungry, they'd give you another one – that impressed me). My mother took me across the street from the hotel one evening and I had my first oysters on the half shell at a place I note is still there.

We did all the things tourists usually do. And I still remember many details from that trip. I suppose it was the most influential trip I ever took. Because after a few days I'd been absolutely seduced by the city. I vividly remember vowing to myself that someday I would live in New York. Twenty-five years later, I did.

And the whole thing was a road trip, though my father was smart enough to just leave the car in the garage while we were in the city. Meanwhile, do you remember your first visit to New York? It wasn't on our high school senior trip was it?

Tomorrow we leave our apartment to Ethan (and his parents and brother who arrived here last night). We'll rent a car and we're off on a road trip.

I haven't owned a car since 1984, though I quite enjoy driving. It's just that living mainly in New York, a car seems more of an aggravation and an expense than it's worth. Parking in a garage in our neighborhood, for instance, is about $600 a month. And you *really* don't want to have to go through the time and enormous hassle of finding parking spaces on the street.

Going to the theater for the evening from our apartment, transportation would cost you $35 if you drove (for parking in the theater district); $18 if you took a cab both ways; or $4 for both ways by subway. In addition, driving would take you longer than either the cab or the subway. That's just one example. People who own cars in New York are either very rich or very stupid – in some cases both.

Terry.

August 23, 2011 - Gilbert, Arizona

Dear Terry,

My first trips to New York occurred when I was seven- and eight-years old, taking the train from Detroit to Grand Central Station in New York, and then riding in a cab to Oradell, New Jersey where my grandparents lived.

I have Nabokovian ... almost Proustian memories of the beauty of those travels because the train ride was so magical. In fact, when asked in recent years to do a closed-eyes visualization of a "favorite place" I always chose being in the sleeping car of that train to New York, watching the night scenes flash by in the window. (A visualization like that with your eyes closed will take your brain waves from their frenzied, left-brain beta state into a peaceful alpha wave state, a great place to rejuvenate in, even for 20 seconds.)

In your youth you were always more determined than I was. (Though I made up for it later, after I sobered up and realized that I'd wasted my life intoxicating myself, as a child with lazy pleasures, and as an adult with beverages.) That you chose early to one day live in New York impresses me

As a child it was the traveling there that I loved most about New York. Then, when you and I and our senior class took the class trip to New York City and Washington, I was won over. By far the most captivating city in the world ... one of the reasons why Kathy and I honeymooned there. Once while I was visiting you and Miranda there, and we went out onto the streets headed for some restaurant, you jokingly gestured around to the bustling city and said, "Can you feel that fabled New York energy?" But the truth was that I could!

Steve.

25 August 2011 - Saratoga Springs, New York

S.

This is the first stop on our road trip that will eventually take us to Georgian Bay, Canada.

The racetrack here at Saratoga is known as "the graveyard of favorites." And there have been some historic upsets in this town. Jim Dandy beating the Triple Crown winner Gallant Fox in the 1930 Travers Stakes. Man O War being beaten for the only time in his 20-race career, edged by a colt named, ironically enough, Upset. (Maybe that's the origin of the word?) Perhaps Saratoga's greatest upset, however, was the Americans beating the British at the Battle of Saratoga in 1777 and turning the tide of the Revolutionary War. I think the Americans were like 10 to 1 at the time.

The graveyard thing is largely mythology though. Statistically the same number of favorites win here as anywhere else. Still I was pleased with the myth in the sixth race yesterday when a 9-to-1 shot named Imelda Blue came from dead last at the half mile pole and passed them all to win by half a length. I had a five dollar win bet on her and the proceeds insured me a profit for the day. Hey, I could make a living at this!

We got to Saratoga using Red Smith's famous directions: "Go about 175 miles north, turn left at Union Avenue, and go back about 100 years." After checking into our B&B, we went straight to the Horseracing Hall of Fame where I picked up much of the historical trivia I'm about to download on you now.

Throughout the 1800s the town was a thriving summer resort largely because of the fame and miraculous powers of its "waters." The old waters ploy, as you know, was a very successful hoodwink in the 18th and 19th centuries both in Europe and America. We are much smarter now, of course, allowing ourselves to be sucked in only by much more sophisticated con jobs like copper bracelets, low-carb diets, aroma therapy, feng shui and various New-Agey snake oil salesmen.

Horseracing didn't really start here until the 1860s, but it's a good thing it came along when it did because people were getting wise to the "waters" scam by then. As Red Smith implied, the place hasn't changed that much in the last century or so. If you look at photos of the track and the grandstand from the early 1900s, it looks pretty much as you see it today, except in black and white.

What it is today is – hands down – the prettiest, most race-romance-filled track in North America. Operating only six weeks a year, basically in August, Saratoga serves as sort of a summer vacation for the New York horsemen and their families who spend the rest of the year around New York City at Belmont and Aqueduct. It also features some of the best racing in the country.

The Travers Stakes, which is coming up in two days (unfortunately, we'll be gone by then), is one of the most important races of the year every year. I believe it's the oldest stakes race in the country. Because it's for 3-year-olds and run at a mile and a quarter just like the Kentucky Derby, it's often called the Summer Derby. And it always attracts colts who've run in the earlier triple crown races.

The grandstand is made of wood and the paddock where the horses parade before the race and are saddled and mounted is casual, just a bit of level ground with some grass and a white fence around it. The whole thing feels something like a country fair grounds. Even more so in the morning when they open the track from seven o'clock and you can wander in and watch the morning workouts. They serve a breakfast there, but you can also just get a cup of Starbucks coffee and sit in Mrs. Whitney's box (as I did yesterday morning) and watch the horses fly by. There's even a commentator on the track PA system who tells you who's working out and gives little bits of racing skinny and Saratoga lore. It's all very pleasant.

But no time to tarry, "I'm on the road again." Off to Montreal!

Terry.

29 August 2011 - Dallas, Texas

Terry,

I am in Dallas working with a client on a secret project and not having time to see any of the city or the surrounding area.

But I do recall not long ago being in this city for a job and having time to visit the Texas School Book Depository museum. You get to go to the floor where Oswald was when he shot President Kennedy and even look out the very window to the street below where the presidential limo passed by. In your mind's eye you hoist a rifle up, take a sighting, and see how easy it was to hit the victim.

This reminds me of how quickly we humans turn tragedy into entertainment. This museum in Dallas has added a second floor of exhibits and millions of people have "enjoyed" themselves here touring, joking and learning a little history in the process.

How many people are Civil War nuts, even re-staging the great battles over and over, re-creating the bloodiest times in our nation's history for fun and entertainment? It isn't just this nation, but all over there are Holocaust museums with rides for kids, Jack the Ripper tours of the back streets of London at night. Near where I live there are fun-filled *daily* reenactments of the gunfight at the OK Corral in Tombstone, Arizona.

Tour buses in New York take you to the site of the Twin Towers 9-11 devastation pit as just one small part of the most fun vacation you could ever have.

When Kathy and I toured Washington in one of the buses we heard, "Here's where Lincoln was shot, and here's the barn where John Wilkes Booth hid!" and we all buzzed happily about seeing it.

What fun! What a cool barn!!!! Wilkes hid there! I can't remember having a better time on vacation.

In Montreal I got in touch with a friend, Suzanne Sauvage, who Miranda and I knew from the days we were living in Europe. Suzanne was the head of the Paris office of Burson-Marsteller at that time and she was very welcoming and kind to us there. No less so here in Montreal.

We called her on short notice and asked if we could get together for coffee somewhere. The next morning she picked us up at our hotel and gave us a personal driving tour of the city she obviously loves. She's a native Montrealer and though she's lived in Paris and Toronto at various times, her heart has never left the city on the St. Lawrence. "Toronto has become quite a nice place to live," she told us during the tour, "but the city has no soul."

I lived in Toronto in the 1970s when many Montrealers and English companies, in anticipation of what they thought the growing separatist movement in Quebec would do to business and education in the province, had deserted Montreal for Toronto. Most of these people were Anglo, but there were many French among the transplants too. Regardless of their heritage, however, they all mourned the loss of their city and spoke of Toronto in much the same way Suzanne does.

Montreal *is* a great city. I could happily live there, even in the winter, which is the big negative everyone raises about life there. But I actually like the city in white. They do get quite a bit of snow, much more than we were used to in Toronto.

At one point on the tour, we were driven down through Old Montreal along the road fronting the St. Lawrence River and Suzanne pointed out an office building where she used to work. And even though she did not serve us tea and oranges that came all the way from China, I was able to honestly say "Suzanne took us down to her place by the river."

It is almost impossible for me not to think of Leonard Cohen when I'm in Montreal and, of course, a number of the city's landmarks are mentioned in his song "Suzanne" and others too.

Anyway, this is getting way too long, bye:

Terry.

3 September 2011 - Gilbert, Arizona

Terry,

You are really experiencing Canada! And I too think of Leonard Cohen the moment you mention that Montreal area down by the river.

One thinks of mystical poetic writers like Cohen whose sensual-spiritual ballads are so haunting, as being rather naturally gifted as creators ... people who just flat-out think poetically, and hastily capture their thoughts.

But a friend gave me a book called *Songwriters on Songwriting*, which I highly recommend if only for the amazing Cohen interview, in which he reveals that he works like a laborer on his songs, often writing 60 to 100 verses before choosing the final ones. He said that he and Bob Dylan were having coffee in Paris one morning after a Dylan concert in which Dylan sang Cohen's "Hallelujah." Dylan asked Cohen how long it took him to write it and Cohen said "two years." Cohen then asked Dylan how long it took *him* to write "I and I," a song Cohen particularly liked, and Dylan said "fifteen minutes" and both laughed.

The song you mention, "Suzanne," so eerily beautiful and so lovely to sing, took Cohen many years of work. He had notebooks full of verses that never made it in. And I just loved reading all about his writing methods because sometimes being a great writer is a result of a simple willingness to outwork everyone else. And the whole theme of my professional life has been getting people to see that.

Canadian folksingers Ian and Sylvia sang the lovely *Un Canadien Errant* in French, as did Cohen many years after. You are, these days, *un Canadien errant*. I love reading about your travels there.

I've always wondered why it is that Canada is so musical. Do you have a theory? Great Canadian music people include Neil Young, Joni

Mitchell, Paul Anka, Glenn Gould, Hank Snow, Gordon Lightfoot, The Band, Ian and Sylvia, Anne Murray, Buffy Ste Marie, Barenaked Ladies and list goes on and on!

And I have to say that when K.D Lang sang Cohen's "Hallelujah" during the closing ceremonies of the Olympics in Canada it was the single most moving musical experience I have ever had watching television. Just heartbreakingly beautiful. (Even the Canadian national anthem, unlike ours, is a gorgeous piece of music.)

Love to your traveling partner,

s

ps- Speaking of her, I sent Miranda a Skype text message the other day asking her about the Chinese custom of counting the months in the womb as part of one's age. I'd had a friend who just went to China and said he was shocked to find he was older than he thought over there. Miranda and you just visited there last year, and of course she has ancestry there, but she told me that the womb-counting custom was "old school." This PS relates to nothing, but that's what happens when you are always walking backwards. Linear time and thought mean nothing.

8 September 2011 - South Dakota

Terry,

I am here in Arizona imagining the fun you are having in Canada just about now ... and yes, I know that my e-mail header says "South Dakota," so let me explain that.

I am reading a novel right now that has me situated on a baseball diamond in South Dakota. And it is such a beautifully written novel that I am really at the ball field. Which is something books can do. When they're great

This book is called *The Art of Fielding* by Chad Harbach. I bought it because I'd read so many glowing reviews and I was rather stunned that a book about baseball could be taken that seriously ... Jonathan Franzen, whom I immortalized in my own book *Time Warrior*, said, "First novels this complete and consuming come along very, very seldom."

Franzen also said, "Reading *The Art of Fielding* is like watching a hugely gifted young shortstop: you keep waiting for the errors, but there are no errors."

One of the things I like best about the traveling I do is the time on the airplane when it's just me and my book. There is more delightful solitude and heightened focus for reading during that time than at any other time. But my problem is that there are not a lot of good novels anymore. Not to my subjective liking anyway. I am more picky than ever. But this book is a rare exception.

Don't you agree that books are a means of traveling? More so even than movies because the right side of the brain has to *create* the scene that the left side is dutifully reading about, whereas a movie just sort of washes over the senses.

When we were younger, both about 10 years old, it was you who got me hooked on reading. My parents had always recommended it, but I never saw my parents as being the source of fun ideas. So I ignored them. But when you urged the Oz books on me, I became hooked on reading and never let up. Because you *were* a source of great fun, then as now.

Love to Miranda, s.

21 Sept 11 – Georgian Bay, Ontario, Canada.

s.

We are now here at the end of our road trip for a month's stay in the woods on Georgian Bay in the same cottage we've spent the last ten autumns. A bit empty this year because of the missing dog Samson who used to allow us to take care of and love him during our annual six-weeks' stay here. He died earlier this year and I must say we miss him.

I write "Georgian Bay" as my location because we are in the woods by the lake and not in any official town. But that would not really help you locate us were you, say, Stanley and I, say, Livingstone. If you look up Georgian Bay on a map you will discover it is a part of Lake Huron, and not an insignificant part. About 160 miles long and 60 miles wide at its widest, the bay is slightly larger than the state of Connecticut. It contains more than 30,000 islands, some of which come and go from year to year depending on water levels.

So, to be more helpful to you, Stanley, let me tell you we are on the southern end of the bay. The nearest town, about four miles away is called Lafontaine. A variety store, a Catholic church, a liquor store, a hockey rink. Population, 400.

The closest town of any size is maybe 10 miles distant. Penetanguishene: several variety stores plus a supermarket, a Catholic church, a liquor store, a hockey rink, one used bookstore. Population, if you believe the sign that announced your arrival in the town, 9,500. It is unwieldy having a town with 15 letters in its name, so it's usually called just Penetang.

We rarely stop in Penetang however because just a few miles down the road is Midland (pop. 16,000). This is the real metropolis of the area: a half dozen variety stores and four supermarkets, a United Church (Midland is predominantly English-speaking and Protestant while Penetang and Lafontaine have large French-speaking Catholic populations), a liquor store, a movie theater (!), a sex shop, a hockey rink and *three* used bookstores.

Poking around in one of the Midland used bookstores – a musty, unorganized warren of a place – I came upon, and bought, a Graham Greene travel book of sorts. It comprised two journals Greene kept on visits to Africa. A trip to the Congo in 1959 and one in 1942 to West Africa for government work.

Early on in this small book, Greene mentions a truth about travel that I have noticed myself. Travel, by its very nature, is a break in your day-to-day life. You cannot fall back on your accustomed routines, routines you may not have even noticed you've developed. What Greene notes is how quickly on a trip you develop new routines to take their place. Maybe this is an indication of a basic human need for routine. I wonder if this happens with you, your trips being generally so much shorter. But for me, even if I'm in a place only a few days, I'll find myself attached to new routines.

We're on Georgian Bay for more than a month each fall and the new routines establish themselves quickly. In New York and Mexico I almost never have anything more than coffee for breakfast. Here, every day Miranda makes me a slice of rye toast, buttered, with a generous slab of aged Ontario cheddar on it. It is so good I wonder that I don't have it when I'm elsewhere in the world – and yet it remains a Georgian Bay-only treat.

We've also developed a Sunday routine. We have no television up here, so on Sundays we drive about 25 miles round trip to a sports bar called Boston Pizza to catch a part of either the Giants or the Jets football game, or, if the timing works out, a quarter or two of each. We always order the same things: dried, salt and peppered, pork riblets; "hot" baked chicken wings; a pot of tea for Miranda and a pint of Canadian beer for me. "Canadian" here is not used to distinguish it from "American" or "German," it's actually a brand name – Molson Canadian.

We also drive into town (usually the closest, Lafontaine) each day to pick up a newspaper, which we do not read until the next morning at coffee. As a result, we are always a day behind in our news. If the U.S. decides to invade yet another country while we're up here, Miranda and I won't find out about it until two days after D-Day.

So yes, we are a bit isolated up here. After Labour Day, the cottagers tend to stay in Toronto and we pretty much have the woods and the beach to ourselves. It's not something I really notice however. For instance it wasn't until I write you now that I realize that yesterday, despite taking our usual three mile walk on the beach in the morning and spending some time on the lake in the afternoon, we did not see a single other person all day – outside of the guy I bought the paper from in Lafontaine and may have spent 15 seconds with.

Canadians are very defensive about preserving "Canadian culture" in a way that Americans never are about "American culture."

I must say the Canadian fear is not without justification. This is a country with 90% of its population living within 50 miles of the most influential culture in the world; this is a country with a population one-tenth of its nearest neighbor, which happens to be the most influential culture in the world; this is a country whose population spends a majority of its TV-viewing time watching programming from another country, one which happens to be the most influential culture in the world.

The preservation of Canadian culture involves defining it in the first place. And I'm afraid there's no real consensus as to what elements make up this culture. The country's intellectual elite argue that Canadian culture is all about painfully slow-moving films, a Group of artists from the early-to-mid 1900s that *not one* non-Canadian in the world has ever heard of, a body of literature dealing with survival in the woods, and the importance of pronouncing the last letter of the alphabet "zed" rather than "zee."

Personally I'd pitch true Canadian culture a bit lower. I think it has a lot to do with the kinds of things my new friends at Den's Skillet care about: Hockey. Winter. And Tim Hortons. Of course, Canada's highbrows won't like my definition, but it seems to me that these elements (along with the French presence) are the things that distinguish Canada from the United States.

I know you're familiar with hockey and with winter from your days growing up in Michigan, but you may not know Tim Hortons. It's a chain of more than 3000 coffee shops in Canada that absolutely own the country. The latest numbers I saw showed Tim Horton's with 62% of the coffee market with second place going to Starbuck's with 7%. The product itself is either "much better than" or "not as good as" Starbuck's, depending on whether you're Canadian or American. The chain is named after, and was started by: that's right … a hockey player.

The central place hockey holds in the country's psyche was brought home to me by the death of Maurice "the Rocket" Richard, the Montreal Canadians' super goal-scoring winger from the 1940s and '50s. He'd been out of hockey for 40 years when he died in May of 2000, and yet he was given a nationally televised state funeral. The Quebec legislature closed for the day and it was estimated that 115,000 people attended the funeral. Among the mourners were the Prime Minister of Canada and the Governor-General. The Montreal Expos, a *baseball* team you may recall, wore Richard's hockey number 9 in black on their sleeves the entire 2000 season.

I wonder how many people will show for Barry Bonds' funeral.

t.

30 September 2011 - Scottsdale, Arizona

Terry,

Random thoughts: I am inferior. I'm a loser. Compared to you. As a traveler. My travels take me to where? Paris? The Orient?

No, Scottsdale.

From Gilbert to Scottsdale. I sit in Scottsdale in my car typing on my iPad. I am here to give a seminar. Your father told me before he died that I should be a teacher. I couldn't see it at the time. He could. I knew I'd never survive the lengthy accreditation and certification process sometimes known as upper education. How could I have? I studied beer, music and drugs at the University of Arizona. Barely made it through the undergrad programs. Took me 12 years of manic devotion to a single academic goal.

But then I certified myself. I took the free enterprise route. You don't need credentials. Lucky for me. Just a little moxie and a passion for teaching. Your father saw that. He smiles down. He was always a hero to me.

But sometimes that lack of education comes back to bite me. For example, I had to look up the word *quotidian* ...a word you used freely with me as if I were a fellow University of Michigan grad.

Turns out the Latin *quotidianus* means "daily." (I slap my forehead because I took Latin in high school and plum forgot that word!). So you talk now about "living our daily lives." (I substituted "daily" for "quotidian" so I could get my mind around it.) But you, sir, have no normal daily life! Not as the rest of us know it.

For example, I always have to ask where you are. Whenever I call or email, I have to ask you to remind me what country you are in. France? Italy? Canada? Mexico? The Village? And this, I know, is by design. So that you can stay awake to life while the rest of us nod off.

I like your prescriptions for narcolepsy. I have my own. I like to push myself in absurd ways. To make up for my first forty some years of sleepy laziness, I have written or co-written over 30 books, over 30 songs, many published poems. I give speeches and seminars. I take singing lessons. I am not bragging. I am prescribing, too, because anyone can do this, which is why I also teach it. I teach people to write poetry, sing and dance, and create wealth while doing so. These are my own prescriptions. Laugh, too. I say LSD, Laughing, Singing and Dancing across the planet.

You mention the Maple Leafs. As you'll remember, our own high school team was the Birmingham Maples. Our colors were deep maroon and snowy white. Kathy once attempted to make fun of our nickname, the Maples. But I pointed out that Toronto's hockey team is the Maple *Leafs* and no one thinks they're wimps. And if a Leaf is powerful enough, how about the mighty Maple tree itself? A very strong nickname, I argued.

I remember Rocket Richard, and even his lesser brother they called the "Pocket Rocket." You and I were lucky enough to grow up outside Detroit in the heyday of great hockey and see stars like Gordie Howe, Jacques Plante. Jean Beliveau, and Ted Lindsay. That's the last I ever followed hockey. I think Arizona has a team called the Coyotes but I've yet to see them play. One must choose. One can't follow everything.

You are the Rocket of world travel. I am attempting to be the Pocket Rocket.

Love to your French-speaking travel companion, S.

30 Sept 11 – Georgian Bay, Canada

Steve,

There is a once well-regarded writer from the first half of the last century named Hillare Belloc. Have you ever heard of him? Hardly anyone has these days. And having read a book of his writings several years ago I can tell you with assurance the reason why: his writing style is extremely dated. But I remember very clearly a passage in one of his essays about two possible ways to live your life:

One was to travel to the four corners of the earth to see everything everywhere. The other was to spend your entire life living in the same place and to study it, to know and appreciate it in great depth. He makes no judgment as to which is the right way to live; in fact, he suggests that either of those extremes is the best.

There are, as you point out, more ways than one to keep from falling asleep. And that's the objective, isn't it? Not the number of countries visited.

On the other hand, I was struck when I realized that I have lived at least a cumulative year in five different countries. I believe you can only count two. With any luck at all over the next five years, I'll probably be able to add Spain to my total.

But even as I congratulate myself on my travel resume, I know that Miranda is already one country ahead of me and that she'll remain so even when we pick up Spain because we'll do it together.

I used the word quotidian, by the way, more in the sense of "everyday" or "commonplace" rather than meaning "daily." But when you substituted "daily" I was forced to run to a dictionary (one, incidentally, that my father gave me when I was still in university) to see if I'd been forever using the word sloppily.

Thankfully for my peace of mind, I found support for both of our uses there. Certainly the meanings are close anyway, but it does seem to me that there are shadings of difference and I'd hate to think I wasn't really saying what I *thought* I was saying all these years.

The Irish poet Paul Muldoon, who you once met on the corner of Bleecker and Thompson in Greenwich Village, wrote a book of poems I quite enjoyed called *The Prince of Quotidian.*

t.

4 October 2011 - Farmington, New Mexico

Dear Terry,

It's amazing to me how many cars were on the road in the pitch dark of a 4:30 am Arizona morning! Where were they going?

This morning I woke up ultra early to be ready to drive from Gilbert, Arizona to Deer Valley, Arizona, where I would get into a small company plane that would take me and three of my clients to Farmington, New Mexico, in time for a daylong seminar.

Actually, summers (which extend into early October) in Arizona are so hot that anyone who can start their day at 4 or 5 does. Especially people who work outdoors. I saw a lot of trucks and pickups as I drove to the Deer Valley airport. In the eerie beauty of the black morning I made it more eerie by listening to the end of George Noory's "Coast to Coast" radio show. The show is famous for focusing on UFOs, the paranormal, and anything else that might go bump in the night. George's guest this dark-as-outer-space morning was physicist and parapsychologist Russell Targ. Targ discussed a book he co-authored, *The End of Suffering,* and also recounted some of his remote viewing experiences.

You wrote to me in *Two Guys Read the Obituaries* about Johnny Carson's great Carnac routines in which he holds the envelope to his forehead and then guesses its contents. That's called "remote viewing." If I were skilled in remote viewing I could see you now on Georgian Bay on your power walk, pacing along the beach. The military is said to use remote viewing practitioners, yet strangely none of them were able to tune in Osama bin Laden.

Targ, however, links the whole ESP thing to being willing to give up the ego and feel our true spacious connection to everything. The great web of life. As I drive down the road listening to him, the universe opens up and invites me into its emptiness.

It was during Targ's experiments at the Stanford Research Institute that he first caught on to the idea that he was more than just a physical body. Later, while working for Lockheed Martin, he noticed that engineers tended to die within three years of their retirement. (Oh no! How long have you been retired? No, we've discussed that already. You are MORE active in your retirement than you were in your work life, and have the meticulous journal entries on writing time, poems read, walking time, etc. to prove it.) Targ concluded that retirees had lost the "idea of themselves" and that their lives had been overly defined by their work. His grief over the untimely death of his daughter Elisabeth prompted him to examine more deeply the nature of his own suffering. And how to end it.

As the sun came up we flew across Arizona into New Mexico, looking down at vast stretches of mountains and desert and then through the clouds to the greener, more watery terrain of the picturesque San Juan River Valley in New Mexico. Farmington is within sight of Colorado's San Juan Mountains as well as the desert highlands of Arizona and Utah.

That's why the power plant that I'm visiting is called Four Corners: it's located right where the four corners of Colorado, Utah, Arizona and New Mexico converge. The Four Corners area is legendary for its year-round refreshing climate. I daydreamed about creating a retirement community here. It's perfect. (Except that retirees would be dead in three years.) Developers take note.

The five-unit, 2,040-megawatt Four Corners Power Plant, located on the Navajo Indian Reservation west of Farmington, New Mexico, is operated by Arizona Public Services (APS) a client of mine for 15 years! I've been training their leaders and employees in communication and leadership, and I've enjoyed every minute of it. This particular plant I'm speaking at is fueled by low-sulfur coal from the nearby Navajo mine. Nearly 80 percent of the employees at the plant are Native American. One time during a visit one of the Native Americans told me they were impressed that I'd quoted a Navajo proverb in one of my early books: "You can't wake a man who is pretending to sleep." That proverb says it all. As far as I'm concerned.

The Cessna Chancellor we flew in is a little small for me. Not that I have great fear, but I get butterflies in a twin-engine prop that "safely and comfortably accommodates up to five passengers" according to the little promo sheet I found next to the air sickness bag. (I had to email my weight to the pilot last week prior to flight.) I couldn't get the Amelia Earhardt song out of my head as we were landing, but the view was breathtakingly beautiful.

Four Corners delivers power through its switchyard to utilities in Arizona, California, New Mexico and Texas. Cooling water for all five units comes from the man-made Morgan Lake which sits right next to the plant. Oddly, this lake is beautiful as the sun comes up and throws deep pink and orange paint streaks across the water. I love power stations and man-made lakes. (I would not be someone Al Gore bonded with right away, though I'm sure once he got to know me we'd be chums.) And maybe some of that is because these people are paying me to be here and talk to them. But I'm not sure. They do this external stuff so well: the lit-up towers of megapower. They only need my help with the internal: the interior journey: the bridges and power stations of the mind.

Steve

5 Oct 2011 – Georgian Bay, Canada.

Steve,

I'm still here on Georgian Bay. Haven't taken any new trips so I guess I have no right to write you, but I'm worried. You gotta get out of the West; there's something in the air out there and you've caught it.

You're going soft on me, Steve, paying attention to guys who see Martians. Come on, take a trip to sanity; take a trip East.

T

11 October 2011 - Tucson, Arizona

Terry,

We drove down to Tucson today to attend a funeral in the desert.

Tita Knipe was our friend Fred Knipe's mother, and kind of my own mother, too, when I came to Arizona from Michigan back in the 1960s. She always made me feel loved, and always so welcome in her cozy home. She had a playful warmth that was spiritual in the true sense. She could challenge my ideas and love me all the more if I disagreed with her. Will we ever see anyone like her again? I can assure you we won't.

You and I wrote a book about obituaries (*Two Guys Read the Obituaries*) but never in our year of studying that journalistic form have I ever encountered an obit as beautiful as this one. And this glorious writing was obviously inspired by the wonderful person whose life it describes:

"Edith Counter Knipe, 96, mother, sister, daughter, gardener, pioneer, reader, teacher, linguist, activist, stylist, pianist, conversationalist, guardian, friend and provocateur. Also known popularly as Tita, she was a chariot lynchpin and the major branch of an extensive family tree whose tap root descends deeply below this community. Born at St. Mary's Hospital in Tucson to immigrant parents, she lost her father in a tragic accident when she was three.

"Her mother, Eleanor, alone sustained her and her sister, Genevieve, through the Great Depression by hard work and unflagging faith before marrying her step-father, Harry A. Sellers, in the 1930s. At that time an officer with the Arizona Highway Patrol, Harry gradually improved his family's fortunes through real estate acquisition. Tita married a pioneer rancher and architect's son, Frederic Orlando Knipe, Jr., a builder and entrepreneur, shortly after obtaining her English degree at the University of Arizona. She then proceeded to raise five children that survive her, two of which were still dependents at the time of Rick's death in 1969. She subsequently taught school, sold life insurance and worked as a Spanish interpreter until she was 90. She resided for over sixty years at her splendid residence on East Linden Street, a unique dwelling constructed by her husband in 1946. There, she cared for her offspring, counseled the confused and cultivated plants and animals, including a sage and venerable Amazon parrot, Nacho, who presciently passed into bird heaven earlier this year at the age of 50.

"Tita was kind, intelligent and magnetic, invariably at the center of controversy, generally correct in her opinions, and staunchly defensive of her children. Her personal brilliance would have almost been too harsh had it not been secondary to the abundant and constant tidal flow of her love and loveliness. She will be sorely missed, but for all who knew her, the memory of her beauty and magnificence will always be vivid. What, you didn't know her? Well then, believe me, you can really have no idea."

At the services, this Pueblo Indian prayer was passed around:

Hold on to what is good
even if it is a handful of earth

Hold on to what you believe
even when it is a tree
that stands by itself.

Hold on to what you must do
even when it is a long way from here.

Hold on to life
even when it is easier letting go.

Hold on to my hand
even when I have gone away from you.

Steve.

23 October 2011 - Trench Town - Kingston, Jamaica

Terry,

Okay not really in Trench Town. Not even in Jamaica. Just at my friend Carla's house playing guitars and piano and tonight was Bob Marley night featuring *No Woman No Cry* which has us all singing about the poverty-ridden shanty town that was the cradle of reggae, ska and rocksteady music.

I knew the Joan Baez version best of *No Woman No Cry*. So this is my way of saying how wonderfully music can waft us to faraway places with strange sounding names.

Cue up the theme from *My Three Sons*:

Kathy and I recently stayed at the Beverly Garland Holiday Inn in Los Angeles and it was quite charming. Walking distance from Universal Studios. We walked there, but, oh my, it was high on a hill! What a walk!

Beverly Garland was an actress who later owned this hotel. Pictures of her all over, and a nice biodoc movie short running on a continuous loop in the hotel room. Oh, come on, you've heard of her. She starred in *Swamp Women, It Conquered the World* and *The Alligator People* just to name three. Also a ton of TV including *My Three Sons*.

I honestly don't know what part of the world you are in right now, but your next letter or postcard will tell me. We love your postcards. Especially the one you sent from the Vatican with the picture of the Pope with his arms outstretched looking at the crowd. You said he was indicating to the fans the distance short of a first down after a measurement, which it really looked like! You're sure not afraid to take a poke at the Pope.

Did you know that Donovan actually had a song called "A Poke at the Pope?" Okay that's enough traveling music for now … where are you?

S.

24 October 2011 – New York, NY

s.

As indicated above, we're in New York right now and loving it. The only bad thing about our travel-packed calendars is how little time we actually get to spend in what we consider to be our home and is clearly the greatest city in the world. This time, for instance, we'll only be here for seven more days and then we're off to Mexico on November 1ˢᵗ.

Still we try to pack everything we can in while we're here. During our stay we'll see three plays, visit a half dozen museums (I saw the new deKooning retrospective at the Museum of Modern Art twice) and eat at as many restaurants, a mix of old favorites and new ones.

Music as transport.

It's true that you can travel through songs. But a twist on the reverse is also true: often my truest and most poignant memory of a place comes from the music I first heard there. Sometimes it is music indigenous to a place, but it can also be music that's just attached itself to a country, a city or even a room for me. Usually because it was the first place I heard it or because I simply listened to it a lot there.

For instance, are you familiar with fado music? I had no knowledge of it until we visited Portugal where it is traditional and sung in many of the Lisbon night clubs. It has been compared to the blues, but I gotta tell you it's way more mournful. There are upbeat blues songs, optimistic blues songs. Songs that basically say: yeah, it's a bit rough right now but I'll be back on my feet someday; or, my baby's gone, but there might be another one around the corner. Songs like "San Francisco Bay Blues" definitely have a happy feel.

There are *none* of those songs in fado. After hearing a fado song you feel you have to put the singer on suicide watch. Each song is about ineffable loss. My baby's gone, where's my arsenic?; or my friends have deserted me, let's see if I can remember how to make a noose; or the sun just went down, thank goodness my pistol's loaded. It's rugged, Steve.

On the other hand, you can spend a great evening going to a night club or a café in the Bairro Alto district of Lisbon, drink a few glasses of port and listen to a fado singer for a few hours. You come out of there knowing that no matter how bad your life is, it can't begin to compare with the misery of the singer's. Quite cathartic.

So every time I hear a fado song now I walk the streets of Lisbon again in my mind. And that's logical right? A distinctly Portuguese music takes me back to Portugal. But what about the fact that whenever I hear any of the Cuban music from the famous Buena Vista Social Club album I am transported to Paris not Havana?

You could say it's because I've never been to Havana, but that lack of familiarity didn't stop you from traveling to Trenchtown, did it? No, the reason my mind goes to Paris is that during the three years we lived in Paris, we played the Buena Vista Social Club album hundreds of times. Those tunes are in the Paris air for me, much more than something more obvious like "La Vie en Rose" or "Zank 'Evan for Leetel Garels" (not sure of the spelling of that).

The effect is the same as Proust's madeleine – an involuntary evocation of a specific place and time in my memory. I assume it's like that for everyone; I can't believe we're the only people in the world with that kind of attachment to music.

The first Beatles' album, the one with the four seemingly disembodied heads on the cover, takes me to the room called the Sophomore Suite in Deke house at Michigan in 1964. The first Joan Baez album, the one with the song "Mary Hamilton" on it, takes me to your living room in Bloomfield Hills, Michigan, in 1962. Okay, enough of this, I could certainly document my life as a mix tape, but I'm not sure it would make it any more interesting to anyone but me.

Let me just add one travel-music story. In about 1988 Miranda and I went down to Jamaica. We didn't go to Trenchtown; we weren't in the "gritty-Jamaica" mood. Instead we went to a luxurious resort near Montego Bay on the other end of the island. The resort was somehow linked with Noel Coward (he'd stayed there? ... he was an original investor in the hotel? ... he'd once played the piano there? ... someone thought he'd once seen a guy that looked like him there? ... Something.) And the place was certainly not nervous about cashing in on this connection, whatever it may have been.

The bar had pictures of him on the walls. The muzak had his songs floating through the jasmine-scented air ("Only mad dogs and Englishmen go out in the midday sun" etc.) The setting was beautiful; the hotel was beautiful; the maids and the waiters were beautiful.

The place was deserted.

There weren't more than five or six couples in the entire place which had a hundred or so rooms. Well, first off it was off-season; apparently no one goes to Jamaica in July. But also the hotel had been closed for renovation for a year or so and was just re-opening. They had done a "soft" re-launch to prepare themselves and train the staff for the heavy tourism season in the winter. Anyway Miranda had found this bargain and we pretty much had the place to ourselves and, frankly, we were loving it.

We would have dinner on the terrace or on the beach and we'd be the only people there, except for the four or five hovering waiters and busboys ... plus the two musicians playing, basically, Harry Belafonte's greatest hits – "Jamaica Farewell," "Matilda," "The Banana Boat Song" (aka "Day-O")." One guy played guitar and the other the bongos. They were virtually our own private minstrels – no one else was in the dining room or on the beach when we were eating there.

On the third or fourth night, I asked if they could do the Bob Marley song "I Shot the Sheriff." They immediately replied that they did not know that song. Miranda asked for "No Woman No Cry" and for "One Love." Same response from the Calypso-istas. They claimed they didn't know a single reggae song. This was obviously not true.

Marley and his songs were known by everyone in Jamaica. When he died a half dozen years before this, the Prime Minister of Jamaica spoke at his funeral. The "Legend" album (1984) which had all his greatest hits had gone ten times Platinum in the United States.

Clearly what had happened was that the resort management and the tourism people from Montego Bay had told the musicians that they couldn't play reggae for tourists. This, you'll remember was when reggae was thought to be dangerous music associated with violence, marijuana and very scary looking hair styles. So for the rest of our stay we heard Belafonte covers with our dinner.

The irony is that about a year later, the Jamaica Tourism people ran a heavy television advertising campaign in the eastern United States all based around the Bob Marley song "One Love." Obviously somebody with some brains had come to a position of power. A rare occurrence in *any* government bureaucracy.

t.

October 31, 2011 - Chicago, Illinois

Terry,

Chicago is cloudy and windy and we were on a boat today doing one of the "architecture tours" up and down the Chicago river and out onto Lake Michigan, taking in the skyscrapers and hearing all the stories about the Fire and the rebuilding of Chicago. I knew this tour existed because of the movie *The Breakup* wherein Vince Vaughan played a tour guide on one of these very boats.

Notice how movies affect our travel.

The movie *Return to Me* was filmed in Chicago in 1999 and Kathy has seen it many times. It's a heartbreakingly romantic film starring David Duchovney and Minnie Driver. Minnie has literally just received a heart transplant, and I won't give away the rest except for the fact that most of it is filmed in a charming little restaurant, where, of course we went to eat. It's called the Twin Anchors. Turns out Sinatra used to eat there. He would always order their famous ribs (which I ordered) and the story was that he would say to the waitress, "Ribs ... and keep 'em comin'!" This little story was on the menu and I was tempted to say the same thing but I did not, and I was glad because one huge serving was more than enough.

Tom Wolfe, in an essay about Marshall McLuhan years ago described a "digital civilization, in which all humanity will be wired up and online so that geographic locations and national boundaries, or so it's predicted, will become irrelevant."

And in a way this has happened. Because we went to the Lincoln Park zoo (which I had already seen in movies), and this zoo, like the whole Chicago scene, was extremely familiar from digital sources, like movies and TV.

But just how "real" is a movie? Or a live streaming video cam on my computer just now? Or Skype? I often work with clients now on Skype, and they may be in London, England, but they are LIVE to me on my screen in the office! Am I actually seeing and experiencing them in London itself?

If a tree falls in the forest, and no one is there, does it make a sound? I have always wondered about the IQ of people who ask that question and then get that faraway metaphysical look in their eyes as if pondering a deep zen koan. Of course it does *not* make a sound if there is no one there, because "sound" is a vibration's interaction with a human or animal's ear. With no receptor ear to capture the vibration and translate it into "sound" in one's brain, there is no sound. Is that so hard to understand?

But here's where it gets interesting for me. My experience of you, on voicemail is a result of my ears hearing a vibration made originally by your voice. Your voice vibration was "captured" by the voicemail receiver and now I play it and it sounds exactly like you sound when you are "really" there.

If we get more technical, it's not the "real" you I hear even when you are live at the other end of the phone. It's an electronic transmission of your vibration made at the point of origin.

Welcome to a digital civilization in which my travel reports are more about the *movies about Chicago* than they are about Chicago itself. (Although most of that is because I am such a poor descriptive writer.)

Take enough LSD and a movie can be experienced as *more* real than reality. (Certain films, like *Alligator People* or *The Exorcist,* are films you never want to see while on acid.)

I hear you are going to Veracruz now where there have been a huge number of murders and beheadings. So I may want to experience Veracruz in a safer way, by watching the Gary Cooper movie *Vera Cruz.*

I have received a lot of criticism over the years for a chapter in my book called the *17 Lies*. It's the chapter called, "It's a Shame We Didn't Capture That on Video" and it's about how we often try to upgrade reality by putting it on video instead of just experiencing it. People who loved videotaping their children's every movement hated me for that chapter.

I quoted Norman Mailer saying, in very grumpy tones, "The American family travels to strange places in order to take photographs and bring them back, as if the photographs will serve in future years as data-points, crystals of memory to give emotional resonance to experience that was originally without any."

So I guess I am on record in favor of LIVE reality over the digital reproduction. And I know you are; otherwise why else travel as you do? You could just watch Gary Cooper movies.

One of my competitors in the corporate training world once trained a team of surrogates to deliver his seminars so his greed could be more fully experienced. When a client of mine asked if the training his trainees did was any good, I disparaged it by calling it "Inflatable woman training."

You could buy that training or you can hire (me) the real thing.

They say never run down your competitors, but I've always ignored that (and most other) rules of good salesmanship. That could be why I am still having to work at the age of 66.

When you are in Veracruz please wear the titanium energy necklace I sent you (the one we wrote about in our baseball book.) They are very hard to cut through.

Love to Miranda,

S.

2 Nov 2011 – San Miguel de Allende, MX

Steve,

We just flew down here yesterday and I picked up your Chicago visit e-mail in which you mused on the role of films in travel.

I've always liked Chicago. To me it seems the only city in the Midwest worth visiting ... unless you have close relatives in the vicinity of another. And yes, I've taken, and loved, the architectural boat tour there and always recommend it to anyone going there. I'd have done the same for you if you hadn't sneaked off to that toddlin' town without letting me know you were going. But I guess Vince Vaughn let you in on the secret.

Though I took the tour about 15 years ago, I still remember many of the lecture points that were made: The Chicago Fire. Louis Sullivan, "the father of skyscrapers." The brilliant idea of the hanging walls on a grid, which, along with the invention of the elevator, made skyscrapers possible. Mies van der Rohe being about verticals; Frank Lloyd Wright horizontals. Etc.

You may recall that my first wife was from Chicago originally, and her parents moved back there when we were in college. So I used to visit there quite a bit. The last time I was there was for my 60th birthday. Miranda arranged a little getaway week for the two of us to mark that personal mill stone ... and then surprised me by springing a lot of my near relatives and a celebration on me as a surprise birthday party.

The next day we all went out to the Arlington Park dining room for a day at the races. I don't suppose you went out to Arlington while you were in the city but it really is quite a nice track. And I remember winning money that day so I'm sure you could have done the same. It might have paid for your trip ... or at least the architectural tour ticket.

You wrote about the effect of movies on travel and it's true that there are many cities we know primarily as movie locations. Venice is one. And it's especially true of New York.

I've also found that a movie can make me want to go to a place. I wonder how many plane tickets to New Orleans were bought within 15 minutes of the buyer having seen *The Big Easy*? I have no real recollection of the plot of that movie, but I have a vivid recall of the film's main character, which is clearly the city itself and its music. By comparison the star actor Dennis Quaid is reduced to a mere supporting role.

I went to New Orleans because of that movie and I must say I wasn't disappointed one bit. The city, with its food and music, is unique in the U.S. and would no doubt be one of the most visited cities in the world if it weren't for the unbearable weather, the uncontrolled and unmatched police and political corruption and the unfortunate flight path of Gulf of Mexico hurricanes.

Seriously, it's probably my second favorite city in the country. New York being first, of course.

Another place I made a point of visiting because of a film is Sicily. Several years ago Miranda and I spent about ten days touring the island primarily because we'd seen the Italian movie *The Leopard*. We saw the movie (twice, actually) in turn because I'd been so taken with the book on which it's based. The book remains one of my all-time favorites. But it was the film that really made me want to visit the island.

The movie won the 1963 Palme d'Or at the Cannes Film Festival. (This award has lately been dramatically devalued by giving the embarrassingly pretentious and sleep-inducing *Tree of Life* its honor this year, but forty years ago it used to reward watchable films.) *The Leopard* starred Burt Lancaster in the title role with the rest of the cast being European and many of them actually able to speak Italian. Burt, however, was not. He merely mouthed the words in that language and his lines were later dubbed. Honestly, it was barely noticeable, at least to me.

And that brings up an interesting question. Because I might suggest that the romantic image I've always had of Veracruz is based on having seen, at the age of 10, a movie called *Vera Cruz*. (I'm not sure *why* it was two words in the title because now it's always just one.)

The thing is you referred to that movie as "the Gary Cooper movie *Vera Cruz*" while I have a vivid memory of its being the *Burt Lancaster* movie *Vera Cruz*. I wasn't even sure we were talking about the same movie when you mentioned Gary Cooper being in it.

But, of course, we were both right: *Vera Cruz* starred Cooper *and* Lancaster. Burt really lucked out in this one and was allowed to speak English. The film is about Mexico in the time of the French invasion of this often-invaded country, circa mid-1860s. Veracruz, being the principle east coast Mexican port, has been a favored invader landing spot for almost four centuries – Maximilian and his French army also found it convenient. Anyway, I've always had a vague desire to see this city and I refuse to be put off by the discovery in the last few months of a mere 150 or so executed corpses. That's the kind of intrepid traveler I am!

  t.

13 Nov 11 – Veracruz, Mexico.

Steve,

I'm here in the city of my Burt Lancaster dreams, but apparently he's not here right now. And that whole thing about 150 decapitated bodies lying around seems greatly exaggerated; I haven't seen more than a half dozen or so.

But despite the absence of Lancaster (or Gary Cooper) and the putative presence of an all-out drug war, I gotta believe you'd love this town, Steve.

Because this city seems to exist for music!

You can't walk fifty steps here without bumping into it. In every café, in every plaza, on every street corner – the music is everywhere. To my ear it sounds less Mexican than Cuban. This makes perfect sense when you think about it: Veracruz is Mexico's oldest, largest and historically most significant port. And as a Gulf of Mexico port, its influences come more from the sea than from central Mexico over the mountains. You can hear it in the music; the Caribbean and African rhythms come through loud and clear, transmogrified into a style they call jarocho. (To give you a bit of a sense of the music, the most famous jarocho song is "La Bamba.")

We saw several bands here and typically, if the band has seven members, there will be a singer, a piano player and five percussionists. It's very difficult to simply stand and watch a jarocho band performing. Your feet start dancing. And this city *dances*!

Miranda was sick for one of the three days we were here and that tends to dampen your feeling for a place, but even in her weakened state she loved the town. And she definitely wants to come back and spend more time here.

Speaking of music, the day before we arrived here on this tour, we spent an afternoon in a very pretty, four-syllabled, difficult-to-pronounce town called Tlacotalpan.

The center of this town is almost Disneyland perfect; it's also virtually empty. The beautiful homes here are all owned by wealthy absentee owners who come here for vacations. So for much of the year, the only residents of these impressive houses are the servants. It's very eerie; the place feels like a movie set.

Tlacotalpan's most famous native son is Augustin Lara (1897-1970). In fact his former home is now a museum dedicated to his life. You, given your professional interest in music, probably know all about him, but I felt a bit ignorant not having any idea who he was. Apparently he was not only the composer of more than 700 songs (many of them Mexican classics, including "Granada"), but also sort of the Frank Sinatra of Mexico.

A friend of ours, a woman just a bit younger than I am, who grew up in New York and who was also on the trip, told me that she'd always loved Augustin. I again felt stupid. I mean here's Lara, a Mexican whose songs have been recorded by everyone from Bing Crosby, Nat "King" Cole, Julio Iglesias, Placido Domingo to, well ... Frank Sinatra (the Augustin Lara of the U.S.), how did I miss this guy?

t.

22 November 2011 - Los Angeles, California

Terry,

How great it was today to see you and Miranda at the strange Encounter restaurant at LAX. It was fun having a couple of hours to talk ... and I especially enjoyed hearing about the exhibition you had both seen in Toronto of David Hockney's iPad art!

I went on the internet and Googled him and found his iPad stuff and it was arresting and beautiful, just as you said. I hope everyone reading this will Google Hockney's iPad art.

What an odd restaurant we sat in, though. Up high, looking panoramically out on America's tackiest and most run down and unaccommodating airport. I don't know if LAX is the worst airport in the world, I'll leave that for you to tell me about. But it is the worst in the USA.

This restaurant, The Encounter, looked like a flying saucer on four legs from the outside, and from the inside it had a very cheap-looking, faux groovy retro futuristic decor with lava lamps and uncomfortable space age chairs and tables. I didn't quite get the name "Encounter" until I entered the claustrophobic tiny elevator that took me up to the saucer and heard the imposing sci-fi movie music screeching out of a tinny speaker.

This is where one meets his lifelong friend from childhood and his lovely wife? It was like being on a space journey gone terribly wrong.

I went online to read some reviews of the restaurant and one of the reviewers called it "The Jetsons' version of a greasy spoon."

Of course we overcame everything by making it the object of our sophisticated, razor-sharp wit and always-refreshing mockery. And seeing you was great fun.

As usual.

Love to Miranda, Steve.

23 November 2011 – Los Angeles, California.

Steve,

Miranda once pointed out to me how fun it is meeting up with friends in faraway places. Even somebody who lives just a block away from you at home takes on new intrigue when you bump into him in Rome. Or meet up for dinner in Paris.

So it was a lucky coincidence that you happened to be in Los Angeles (on business) when we were in the city for a family Thanksgiving celebration. And, yes, you've taken on a new exciting persona for me now that I've seen you in this distant city airport. But it is possible that The Encounter (I don't mean to upgrade our meeting to capital letter status, rather I am referring to the name of the restaurant) had a lot to do with the intrigue of the situation. A goofy-looking place. Fun though.

This year, by the way, is the 50th anniversary of the building housing the restaurant and in half a century it's obviously become such a landmark that when we were talking about getting together for a drink and were trying to think of a convenient place, I merely had to describe it to you as that "flying saucer building in the middle of LAX" and you knew exactly what I was talking about.

By the way, the Jetsons television show is mentioned in virtually every review the restaurant has ever received.

t.

28 Nov 11 (at about 4AM Leon time) – on a flight from Los Angeles to Leon, Mexico

Steve,

So far we've written thousands of words about our travels and travelling in general, but neither of us has yet touched on the concept of the infamous "red eye" flight. In my years in advertising I was sometimes forced, by meeting schedules, deadlines or other exigencies, to take the red eye from LA to Detroit, Toronto or New York. After working on an edit or shooting all day in LA, I'd catch a midnight flight east, arriving at 9 or so in the morning and then try to put in a day's work at the office on very little, and fitful, sleep.

It was always a day of torture and I'd rail against the red eye and promise myself never to take another. But then, of course, on the next trip to the west coast, circumstances would cause me to break my promise.

Okay, but that was when I was working and had responsibilities to the agency and clients. So it kind of made sense. What doesn't make sense is why I'm taking one now.

Why did I board this plane in Los Angeles one hour past midnight with an expected arrival in Leon at 6 in the morning? And while we're asking the big questions: Why is this plane full? And why is an overweight woman sitting next to me and overflowing my armrest? And, finally, what are my chances of getting any sleep on this flight?

The answer to the main question is that unfortunately San Miguel is not very easy to get to. There are two options, neither exactly convenient. One is to fly to Mexico City which has a lot of flights that arrive direct from the States and follow that with a four-hour bus ride to San Miguel. The other is to fly to Leon which necessitates only an hour-and-a-half bus ride. Leon, however, is not as popular a destination so there aren't many cities in the U.S. that allow you to fly there direct. The good news is that one of them is LA; the bad news is that there are a limited number of flights … in fact, there's only one. And I'm on it. And I know I'll have bloodshot eyes in the morning.

This section is written later on the same day, after taking a *seven*-hour nap:

I came late to air travel. I was 23 when I took my very first airplane trip – on business to Atlantic City. Because of this I was unfamiliar with the term "red eye" flight. When I first heard it I devised a rather fancifully romantic notion of how the expression came about. Because these flights were at night, I thought the "eye" was the red blinking light you always see from the ground as a plane flies overhead after dark. Like a red blinking eye shooting through the night.

Much later, with some embarrassment at my naïveté, I recognized my error.

I must say I don't really like LA. And yet, how can I say that when I've probably made more than 50 trips there during my life and have to say I've enjoyed every one of them?

I can't.

I will say that I'm baffled by anyone that would live there. For me, it's a great place to visit, but I wouldn't want to live there – just what everyone always says about New York. But seriously, why would anyone want to live in a city where you have to drive *everywhere*? Where half your life is spent on a freeway … in traffic?

LA is also a company town. In the sense that Detroit is or Washington, D.C. Meaning that the town and virtually everyone in it revolves around a single industry. So if you're in Detroit you better care about cars; in Washington, politics; in LA, movies. If you don't, you're going to find yourself a bit out of step and isolated.

The other problem is that the film industry is so lacking in stability, so hit-and-miss and so based on project-hiring that people in the business are constantly fighting to keep up their image. No one wants to hire someone who's out of work, goes the thinking, so no one ever admits that they are out of work; they've always got a "project" going or they're up for some huge movie or a Bud Light commercial.

In another industry, if you lose your job it's a big deal, a crushing blow. But in Los Angeles, if you're *really* successful, you lose your job four times a year – every time a movie you're working on is finished. If you're not successful, you rarely lose your job but rather spend your whole life being turned down for jobs at auditions. This can obviously be very demoralizing to be rejected scores of times each year – especially when outwardly you have to project the image of being very much in demand.

It's a tough life and it leads to the impression of show business people being phonies. They aren't phonies; they're actors – and they're desperate.

Reading this over, I can see where you might think I'm talking just about actors. But I'm talking about everyone in the industry. It's a way of life, and one that doesn't really add up to a very interesting city … for me. But then clearly millions of people disagree with me.

The very first time I came to LA was for the edit of a commercial I had written. I was probably about 24 years old and I asked my secretary to book me a hotel downtown because I wanted to walk around and get a sense of the city.

This was a mistake.

The film business is all around Hollywood and so each morning I had to drive out there to work on the commercial and then I'd stay out there and have dinner, and then each night I'd drive back downtown to spend the night in the hotel. I didn't even have breakfasts at my hotel; I'd go out to where the studio was and have breakfast out there, often with someone I was working with. Being downtown was the LA equivalent of staying in a hotel in the suburbs.

After that experience, over the next 40 years or so, I always stayed out in Beverly Hills, West Hollywood or North Hollywood. I still had to drive everywhere … just not as far.

This last trip with Miranda, however, I got back to my LA roots. We did a house swap with a young woman and stayed in a loft in downtown. Of course, we were in LA for all the family dinners and football game functions surrounding Thanksgiving so we still spent most of our time elsewhere, but we did carve out a bit of time to see some of downtown.

Fifteen years ago this area had a terrible reputation. And rightly so. There were all these big derelict old buildings and thousands of homeless people and Bukowski-type characters wandering the streets. It was not a fun place to go, a bit scary too.

But in the last decade or so, some people with vision have invested in the neighborhood and given it a bit of cachet. Quite a bit, actually. It's now definitely "up and coming." There are lots of art galleries, hip bars and good restaurants and cafes. Meanwhile, a lot of those derelict buildings have been redeveloped into very nice loft apartments like the one we just spent the last week in.

And the homeless population? Well, it's still there but it's down to hundreds rather than thousands. And walking around, you recognize that the rebirth of the area is still a process in progress – one block will be very hip and young and lively and the next will look like a crime scene waiting to happen. (We did see one drug arrest taking place while we were walking around on Saturday evening.)

Going in, I must say we were a bit apprehensive, but by the third or fourth day, Miranda announced that she really quite liked the neighborhood. I did too; it's got a lot going for it. But I could also fully understand people being put off by it, especially people who were used to the Beverly Hills, West Hollywood or Santa Monica parts of the LA area.

A last comment on Los Angeles: Is it possible to take the second largest metropolitan area in the country seriously as a city if it can't even manage to organize a professional football team for itself?

Adios for now,

Terry.

12 Dec11 – San Miguel de Allende

Dear Steve,

I've not written you much about San Miguel de Allende this visit and I wonder why. Some of it is just familiarity. For the last seven years we've been spending about 4-5 months a year down here so I guess I take the place a bit for granted.

I shouldn't, of course, because it's a fascinating and beautiful place. Loaded with legends, uniquely Mexican stories and culture and, for better or worse, this large expat presence. When I say expat, I'm talking mainly Americans, but also a substantial Canadian contingent and more and more Europeans, quite a few French in particular. The expats are not overwhelming in percentage terms; probably 95% of the population is still Mexican. But (again I say it) "for better or worse" the expats constitute much more than 5% of the influence that shapes the town. Much of this due, of course, to economics.

When I first moved from the U.S. to Toronto, Canada, back in 1972, my father told me to write down all my impressions and note all the things that were different. Like most sons everywhere and throughout time, I felt free to ignore my father's advice. And regretted it later.

His point was that things that first struck me as interesting or iconically Canadian or Torontonian would very quickly lose their uniqueness and would simply start seeming commonplace. That, in short, I'd start taking them for granted … like I suppose I've done now with San Miguel.

It's hard to take it for granted today, however, because this is the saint's day of the Virgin of Guadalupe. It's a distinctly Mexican event that this year was first brought to my attention at about 3 o'clock this morning with what might have been the loudest burst of fireworks I've ever heard. The five minutes ringing of the local parish church bells that followed this was like a whisper compared to the fireworks. The sequence, fireworks-bells, was repeated periodically throughout the night. I am an extremely dedicated sleeper and managed to miss the bulk of the explosions; Miranda, however, was wakened by each burst and by morning was thoroughly pissed off with the Virgin.

The Virgin of Guadalupe is technically the same Virgin we all know as Mary. The one that gave birth to Jesus. But she is important in Latin America because she appeared in a vision to an Aztec peasant, one Juan Diego, in 1531 and, pushy as ever, she asked that a church be built in her honor. Well, the story goes on in many different, and sometimes conflicting, versions, but the bottom line is that Juan eventually convinced the bishop to build that church. Most important, the incident marked the first time Mary deigned to be seen by an Indian.

As a result the Virgin of Guadalupe seems to be revered above all other religious figures by the Mexicans and indigenous peoples in many other parts of Latin America. Her importance in Mexico is even greater because her image has political meaning too. It has been used as a rallying standard by two of the country's revolutionary heroes. First in 1810 by the priest Miguel Hidalgo, one of the leaders of the revolution that freed Mexico from Spain, and then more than a hundred years later by Emiliano Zapata who led the fight to end the reign of the dictator Porfirio Diaz and was later played in film by Marlon Brando.

The image of the Virgin is found in virtually every home in Mexico; she is supposed to protect the household. We have two in our house here. All of the markets in Mexico also have altars to Her, again for the purpose of bringing blessings to the place – and more robust sales I suppose.

I think I've told you that I take Spanish three mornings a week at 9 in the center of town. I try to leave 45 minutes ahead of my class so that I can get in my full exercise walk on the way there. If I walked straight to class, it would only take 15 minutes to get there so I've devised a number of circuitous routes to fill out my full exercise walk. My favorite of these is the one that takes me through the San Juan de Dios market. It's the largest market in town with probably 150 to 200 stalls *and* four or five altars to the Virgin of Guadalupe.

I like doing my walk through the market in the morning when the tamales and atole (a hot corn-based morning drink) sellers are getting their custom and the stall keepers are setting up for the day. The neighborhood is very Mexican so it's a real taste of day-to-day life in the city shaking off the cobwebs and coming awake. As opposed to the opening of the Starbucks in town each morning, for instance, which somehow just doesn't seem as authentic despite the fact that everyone working there is Mexican as far as I can tell.

But this morning on my walk through the market I was stopped twice by clusters of Mexicans of all ages standing in front of the Virgin altars singing "Las Mañanitas." This is the traditional saint's day/birthday song.

The celebration continued throughout the city and for the rest of the day I saw elaborate altars to the Virgin put up in various parks and public fountains, more fireworks naturally, and I know of at least three neighborhoods that were hosting full fiestas in the evening. If there's one thing San Miguel can be especially proud of it's its ability to throw a great fiesta. Practice makes perfect.

Adios,

t.

13 December 2011 - Gilbert, Arizona

Terry,

I loved visiting you in San Miguel ... so charming, reminding me of when I was living in Mexico, studying Spanish. I learned then to love the music, and to know that, in the song "Las Mananitas," "El día en que tu naciste nacieron todas las flores. En la pila del bautismo, cantaron los ruiseñores" means, "On the day you were born all the flowers were born. On the baptismal fountain the nightingales sang."

Spanish is a romance language in more ways than one, no?

S.

24 December 2011 - Gilbert, Arizona (no snow)

Terry.

Merry Christmas to you wherever you are in the world ... I have lost track ...

Is it Feliz Navidad to you? (Best version of that song EVER is on Michael Buble's new Christmas album.)

It's a good old world, is it not? Even though there's a lot of sad stuff and certainly room for improvement and as Dave Barry points out, **"Americans who travel abroad for the first time are often shocked to discover that, despite all the progress that has been made in the last 30 years, many foreign people still speak in foreign languages."**

Love to M,

S.

Christmas – 25 diciembre 2011 - San Miguel de Allende, Mexico

Steve,

You're right; it is a good old world. And I long to see even more of it. Oh well, there's a whole year coming up to add some new spots. Meanwhile we haven't done too badly this year, and I must say I've enjoyed writing you about it all.

Merry Christmas!

t.

About the Authors

Steve Chandler and Terrence N. Hill have been writers all their lives. This book is the fifth in a series that began with the critically acclaimed *Two Guys Read Moby Dick*, followed by the popular *Two Guys Read the Obituaries, Two Guys Read Jane Austen, and Two Guys Read the Box Scores.*.

Chandler has written and co-written over a dozen books, including the bestseller, *Fearless*. He is a professional business coach and corporate trainer whose previous books have been translated into over 20 languages. His blog, iMindShift, is popular around the world, and you can subscribe at his website, www.stevechandler.com. He lives with his musical wife and editor Kathy and good dog Jim on the scenic outskirts of Phoenix in an old house overlooking Vista Allegre Park.

Terrence Hill worked for more than 30 years in advertising beginning as a copywriter and later running agencies in New York and Europe. He has published poetry, essays and short fiction and was the writer for two CBC-TV (Canada) documentary series. In 2005, Terry's play, *Hamlet-The Sequel,* won the Playhouse on the Green (Bridgeport, Connecticut) playwriting competition. You can email Terry at terrynhill@hotmail.com.

Also by Steve Chandler

RelationShift (with Michael Bassoff)

100 Ways to Motivate Yourself

Reinventing Yourself

17 Lies That Are Holding You Back

50 Ways to Create Great Relationships

100 Ways to Create Wealth (with Sam Beckford)

The Small Business Millionaire (with Sam Beckford)

9 Lies that are Holding Your Business Back (with Sam Beckford)

Business Coaching (with Sam Beckford)

How to Get Clients

Two Guys Read Moby Dick (with Terrence N. Hill)

Two Guys Read the Obituaries (with Terrence N. Hill)

Two Guys Read Jane Austen (with Terrence N. Hill)

Two Guys Read the Box Scores (with Terrence N. Hill)

Business Coaching (with Sam Beckford)

The Hands Off Manager (with Duane Black)

The Story of You

100 Ways to Motivate Others (with Scott Richardson)

10 Commitments to Your Success

The Joy of Selling

Fearless

Shift Your Mind: Shift the World

The Woman Who Attracted Money

Robert D. Reed Publishers Order Form

Call in your order for fast service and quantity discounts
(541) 347- 9882

OR order on-line at **www.rdrpublishers.com** *using PayPal.*
OR order by mail:
Make a copy of this form; enclose payment information:
Robert D. Reed Publishers
1380 Face Rock Drive, Bandon, OR 97411
Fax at (541) 347-9883

Send indicated books to:

Name_____

Address _____

City _____ State _____ Zip _____

Phone _____ Fax _____ Cell _____

E-Mail_____

Payment by check ☐ or credit card ☐ *(All major credit cards are accepted.)*

Name on card _____

Card Number _____

Exp. Date _____ Last 3-Digit number on back of card_____

TWO GUYS Series with Terrence N. Hill: *Qty.*

Tho Guys on the Road..$14.95 _____

Two Guys Read the Box Scores..$14.95 _____

Two Guys Read Jane Austen..$11.95 _____

Two Guys Read the Obituaries..$11.95 _____

Two Guys Read Moby-Dick ....$9.95 _____

OTHER BOOKS BY STEVE CHANDLER:

Shift Your Mind, Shift Your World ....$14.95 _____

Fearless...$12.95 _____

The Woman Who Attracted Money...$14.95 _____

The Joy of Selling...$11.95 _____

The Small Business Millionaire (with Sam Beckford)..................$24.95 _____

100 Ways to Create Wealth (with Sam Beckford)........................$24.95 _____

Ten Commitments to Your Success ....$11.95 _____

RelationShift: Revolutionay Fundraising (with Michael Bassoff) ....$14.95 _____

Total Number of Books _____ Total Amount _____

Note: Shipping is $3.50 1st book + $1 for each additional book.   Shipping _____

THE TOTAL_____